SOUTH BELFAST
TERRACE AND VILLA

Paintings by David Evans
Text by Norman Weatherall

Cottage

Publications

First published by Cottage Publications,
an imprint of Laurel Cottage Ltd.
Donaghadee, N. Ireland 2002.
Copyrights Reserved.
© Illustrations by David Evans 2002.
© Text by Norman Weatherall 2002.
All rights reserved.
No part of this book may be reproduced or stored
on any media without the express written
permission of the publishers.
Design & origination in Northern Ireland.
Printed & bound in Singapore.

ISBN 1 90093528 7

Norman Weatherall

Norman Weatherall has lived in South Belfast all his life. He has gained by some of the processes he describes in his text : movement out to new suburbs (though not Malone!), the extension of secondary education to all and the greater availability of university education.

He graduated from Queen's University with an Arts degree and trained as a teacher. His professional life was spent in Grosvenor Grammar School where he taught English and History.

He is a member of the South Belfast Historical Society. With George Templeton he co-authored 'South Belfast' in Gill and McMillan's 'Images of Ireland' series, a collection of old photographs. The South Belfast Community Telegraph has published articles he has written on historical topics relating to Belfast.

David Evans

David Evans is a lecturer in architecture at Queen's University and has lived and worked in South Belfast for most of his life. As an architect his interest lies in the buildings of the area but, in his paintings, he also aims to convey something of the character of the spaces and streetscapes that make up their settings.

He learned to paint with his father Estyn Evans and the work of local artist Tom Carr has been his constant inspiration. He paints in watercolour and is past president of the Royal Ulster Academy of Arts. His work has been commissioned by Queen's University, Trinity College Dublin, the Ulster Museum and the Arts Council for Northern Ireland.

Contents

South Belfast - a Brief History

Although it is not a rigidly defined area, South Belfast is generally considered to be that area of the city and its suburbs fanning out from the City Hall to which structure is given, on the east, by the Ravenhill Road, on the west by the Lisburn Road, with the Malone and Ormeau Roads in between, and stretching out to Newtownbreda, Upper Malone and Finaghy. It embraces 11 city wards.

Townwards, South Belfast occupies slobland (soft clay and marshland) below the post-glacial shoreline. Part was once covered by the Cromac Woods, commemorated today in street names, Oak, Elm, etc., in the Donegall Pass area. The Blackstaff (aka Owenvarra) river meandered across from the west and entered the Lagan at a point roughly where the former Christian Brothers school stands in Oxford Street. Despite the cutting of a new exit for the river at Cromac Dock at the end of the 17th

century the area remained liable to flooding and it would be the early 19th century before land reclamation made possible the Cromac/ Victoria Street developments outlined on a map of 1823; and later still before the 'Blackstaff Nuisance', as it was called, was eliminated from Lower Ormeau.

Above the old shoreline were the Plains, today covered by the University district, the Botanic Gardens and the avenues linking Botanic Avenue and Ormeau Road. The rise in level can be seen, for example, at the head of Bradbury Place where the Lisburn and University Roads separate.

The Malone ridge (variously explained as *Maghluan,* the plain of the lambs, or *Ma Lon,* plain of the elms, or *Maigh Luain,* Luan's Plain) was the best area of all. A moraine deposited by the retreating ice at the end of the last Ice Age, it rose rapidly to 100 feet and offered well

drained, sandy soil to 17th century farmer-settlers and an airy, healthy location for Victorian businessmen to build the grand homes for which they abandoned the old town centre. The ridge falls steeply to the Lagan in the east and gently to the Blackstaff in the west.

The ancient route southwards from Belfast, later the Malone Turnpike, veered to the right at the top of Sandy Row and followed the ridge. A new road, the Lisburn Road, laid out 1817-19, offered a way south that was more direct and had a gentler incline out of Belfast. Users of both roads benefitted from the Abolition of Tolls Act (1857). Since the Lisburn Road attracted both shopping facilities and traffic, the Malone Road was left free to be grandly residential.

The River Lagan (*Abhainn an Lagain,* river of the low-lying district) is a major physical feature of South Belfast, the towpath and boulevards offering pleasant walks to those in search of recreation. The completion of the Lagan Navigation at the end of the 18th century linked the town to Lough Neagh at the heart of the province of Ulster.

The Lagan Valley is not the only recreational space in the area. South Belfast is well endowed with public parks. Belfast's first, Ormeau, was opened in 1871; the Corporation acquired Botanic Gardens in 1895. These have been joined by Cranmore, Musgrave, Barnett's and the Sir Thomas and Lady Dixon Parks, not forgetting Belvoir Forest and the Lagan Meadows.

THE SEVENTEENTH CENTURY

In 1603 James I granted the castle of Belfast and 52 townlands to Arthur Chichester, soldier-adventurer-planter from Devon. In 1606 another planter, Moyses Hill, leased land from Chichester at Malone and Stranmillis and brought in settlers from Lancashire and Cheshire to farm it. This gave an English and Anglican (Church of Ireland) character to South Belfast; in contrast to North Belfast which came to be dominated by Scottish Presbyterian settlers.

Travellers remarked on the attractive nature of Malone. Richard Dobbs, writing in 1683, describes the road through Malone to Belfast: *"From Lambeg the way leads direct to Belfast, which is all along for the most part furnished with houses, little orchards and gardens, and, on the right hand, the Countess of Donegall (of the Chichester family) hath a very fine park, well stored with venison, and in it a horse course of two miles, and may be called an English road."*

At the end of the century the 3rd Earl of Donegall had passages cut through the Cromac Woods as an unemployment relief scheme. The passages were, Henry Joy tells us, *"appropriated to the recreation of the inhabitants of Belfast"*. Two of them survive today as Donegall Pass and (lower) Ormeau Road.

In June of 1690 William III of Orange passed along the Malone Road on his way to fight the battle of the Boyne.

THE EIGHTEENTH CENTURY

The town of Belfast continued to develop on its slobland site and the district that would become South Belfast remained in agricultural use.

At Malone the farms were laid out in strips running from the ridge to the Blackstaff so that each tenant had his share of good sandy soil at the top, boulder clay on the middle slopes and damp meadows at the bottom. This pattern is reflected today in the layout of the avenues between Malone and Lisburn Roads. The farmhouses were close together. Dubourdieu writing in 1812 remarked: *"Nearly all the whole of the Malone Road from Belfast to Lisburn is a village, the houses except where a gentleman's place intervenes, being within call of each other."*

The gentrification of the town's rural fringes began in the later decades of the century with leases to 'gentlemen' replacing those given to farmers. Such leases were a means of investing money at a time when banks might be unreliable and before stocks and shares offered investment prospects. Residence by the early gentlemen leaseholders was at first exceptional and the land continued to be farmed by subtenants. Eventually houses of the type referred to in old-fashioned guidebooks as 'seats' would be built on the land leased.

THE NINETEENTH CENTURY

The assault on the rural fringes by architects and builders, in response to the movement out from the old town and to the increase in population (which would require the boundary of Belfast to be extended several times), did not become really serious until the second half of the 19th century.

Atkinson in his *Ireland Exhibited to England* (1823) could still describe the Malone Road as *"charming, (passing) through demesnes and villas of incomparable beauty, forming one continuous chain of rich plantations from Lisburn to Belfast."* He adds *"The traveller will not see … pigs traversing the roads here. Many inhabitants of the other provinces … cannot protect their lands from being shamefully mangled and defaced by the swine of their poorer neighbours"*. The Irish

Parliamentary Gazetteer of 1846 describes Malone as *"a romantically situated hamlet in the valley of the Lagan"*. Paradise Row, the last remnant of Malone village, close to St. John's church, was demolished c.1900.

From the end of the 18th century to the 1830s Belfast's upper classes resided in terraced houses in Donegall Place, Donegall Square, Wellington Place and College Square. The Rev. Narcissus Batt, who had lived in Donegall Place, remembered it in his childhood (1830s) as *"a quiet street of private houses. Some of them had gardens and trees in the rere, and there was quite a grove at the corner of the square where Robinson and Cleaver now have their establishment"*. The residents were town merchants, professionals, and seasonal visitors who had country houses. But the area was to deteriorate physically and socially. Water supplies and sanitation, Batt tells us, were deficient even in the best houses. Mills and factories using steam power brought *"aerial pollution"*. The influx of people from the countryside changed the social scene. While the town was small, rich and poor had lived in close proximity, but the growing numbers of people made this arrangement increasingly

intolerable. The lower orders did not always know how to behave: Batt witnessed faction fights in Donegall Place; ladies preferred to go to St. George's church in groups on a Sunday evening because High Street could be quite rowdy. By the 1840s people were moving out, businessmen moving in. J. A. Pilson in his *History of the Rise and Progress of Belfast* (1846) explains what was happening: Donegall Place *"formerly the St James' of Belfast…has recently been encroached upon by the enterprising merchants and traders, who have so closely pressed upon the elite as to compel them to retire to the new and more appropriate locale of Wellwood-place, Glengall-street"*, etc. The locations he names were the early stages of South Belfast. Those leaving did so in quest of pleasanter, healthier surroundings. A South Belfast address could provide what they were looking for. Profits from the town's growing industrial and commercial economy paid for the change of residence.

Thus was a framework for South Belfast created. Great Victoria Street and Dublin Road led to University Road (in Denis Ireland's memorable phrase: *"from slobland to snobland"*) where the Queen's College (opened 1849) became a focus for middle class housing. The Malone Road, a short distance away, was to become the grandest address in South Belfast. Emrys Jones called it *"the social successor of Donegall Place"*.

The 'gentlemen's places' referred to by Dubordieu were modest by later Victorian standards. From the 1850s large houses in extensive grounds, Derryvolgie, Danesfort, etc., were being built. The detached villa was the main residential unit; terraces – urban features – were for elsewhere, though a few did get built on the Road, but at the 'town' end. As demand increased, sites became smaller. A kind of Rake's Progress in landholding was enacted: hunting estates/ parks were broken up into ornamental grounds, which in turn were divided into gardens/ shrubberies; the next stage was the minute flower border, then the window box or the aspidistra (indoors) as residents struggled to hold on to something earthy.

Malone's neighbour, the Lisburn Road, followed the line of a lane that linked a number of farms. In 1852 'The Northern Whig' expressed optimism about

residential development there: *"The extension of the suburbs proceeds apace … Perhaps the best arranged 'lot' that we have seen projected is that on the Botanic Road, in the vicinity of the Gardens. The contractors … have already completed some of the houses in a neat and agreeable style … The situation is healthy and rural … The site has obtained the aristocratic name of 'Windsor'."*

The 'extension of the suburbs' was greatly assisted by the establishment of a tramway system, started in 1872, taken over by the Corporation in 1904 and electrified in 1905. The trams made it possible to live in the suburbs and work in the town. Trams were running on the Lisburn Road from 1881, to Hampton Park (Ormeau) by 1885 and to Malone Park by 1888.

South Belfast also enjoyed the advantage of the train. The Ulster Railway opened its first line, to Lisburn, in 1839. Extensions linked Belfast with Lurgan, Portadown, Armagh and Dublin. The Great Victoria Street terminus, built in 1848, was the gateway to a new life for thousands from the countryside seeking work in the

growing town. Stations were opened on the Lisburn Road at Adelaide and Balmoral.

The Stranmillis (from the Irish *sruthan milis*, sweet stream) side of the Malone ridge was built on at the end of the century but the survival of parkland surrounding Stranmillis House meant that development on the east side of the Malone Road was seriously restricted. Stranmillis College now enjoys this open space.

On the eastern flank, South Belfast was extended in the first half of the century in the Markets area (Cromac) by streets of houses in late Georgian style. The movement out of town skipped over the neighbouring unhealthy Blackstaff lowlands. The river was culverted later when Ormeau Avenue was created and working class housing built between it and Donegall Pass. Terraces were erected on the Pass and on the lower Ormeau Road from the 1830s.

The development of the Ormeau Road was assisted by the construction of a bridge over the Lagan, 1815, so that travellers no longer had to use the Old Ballynafoy (Ravenhill) Road and the Long Bridge to reach the town. This brought the village of Ballynafeigh within the orbit of Belfast.

Financial constraints had brought the 2nd Marquess of Donegall to live in Belfast. At his death in 1844 he left the estate deeply in debt. The family made use of the Encumbered Estates Act to raise money, in the process freeing much land in South Belfast for building.

The great increase in population, in 1900 five times what it had been in 1840, fuelled a building boom which peaked in the 1890s. As a result many gaps in South Belfast were filled with streets of houses.

THE TWENTIETH CENTURY

South Belfast continued to grow, though two world wars and the depression of the '30s affected the number of houses built. A look around, say, the avenues between the Lisburn and Malone Roads reveals infill housing dating from between the wars. Ribbon development took the Lisburn Road out to Finaghy and beyond.

In 1936 the 'Belfast Telegraph', under a photograph of one of Malone's great houses, lamented *"another beautifully situated old Belfast estate … has bowed to the onward march of the modern builder"*. In the same year McMaster's Estates were offering detached villas on the Dorchester Estate, Upper Malone, three reception rooms, four bedrooms, tiled bathroom, brick garage and a maid's room off the kitchen for £1050.

That classes were no longer being separated by place of residence is suggested by the appearance of Corporation housing in 1923 off the Stranmillis Road and after World War II the working-class estate of Taughmonagh was built at Upper Malone.

Post war the housing stock in many areas of the city was found to be seriously sub-standard and new estates were created under the direction of the Housing Trust, later the Housing Executive. As a result South Belfast has gained by the addition of the Belvoir Park and Milltown estates, causing another movement out. Re-development took place in Cromac and Donegall Pass and 'pre-fab' Taughmonagh has been rebuilt in brick. Some of the

older housing has been improved by the addition of new kitchens and bathrooms.

Malone continues to attract new houses and blocks of apartments are being squeezed in wherever possible, witness the fate of Broomhill at the junction of the Stranmillis and Malone Roads and the new apartments at Danesfort, Malone. At the same time the cleaned-up Lagan has won recognition as an asset and smart apartments have appeared overlooking the river on the Ormeau Embankment, at the Albert Bridge and at Stranmillis.

For many the motor car has taken over from public transport with the result that people are choosing to live ever further out of town. South Belfast's tentacles are stretching out to seize more and more of the countryside. The Matthew Stop Line is a distant memory. Those who deplore the builder's apparently insatiable appetite for green field sites might take a little comfort from the building of 'luxury' apartments in South Belfast close to the City Hall and the conversion of redundant industrial premises to the same use. After a century of moving out it seems that there is now a moving in.

The 3rd Earl of Donegall, landlord of Belfast, had three 'passages' cut through the Cromac Woods in the 1690s as an unemployment relief scheme. Donegall Pass was one of them. Its residential development dates from the 1830s.

Beside St. Mary Magdalene Church is Apsley Place (1846), eight houses in late Georgian style, the grandest terrace on the Pass.

An Ulster History Circle plaque on number 62 commemorates Mary Ann McCracken, who died there in 1866, aged 96. She was the sister of 1798 hero, Henry Joy McCracken. The inscription on her tombstone in Clifton Street graveyard tells us that she *"Wept by her brother's scaffold"*. But her claim to be remembered has a more substantial foundation.

Her fame rests on her record as a social reformer, her work finding its focus in the Belfast Chartiable Society (aka the Poor House) which is perhaps not surprising since she was the niece of two of its founders. For many years she was secretary of the Ladies Committee.

The Poor House was managed by men; the Ladies Committee, chiefly interested in the women and children in the House, could only recommend. As secretary, Mary Ann was the link between the two parties. There is a reasonableness about her letters that would have been difficult to ignore. For example, her presentation of the case for giving the nursery children sweet milk instead of the (cheaper) buttermilk: *"The gentlemen are no doubt aware that there is but little nourishment in buttermilk."* The gentlemen could only agree.

The elimination of vermin in the Poor House, the setting up of an infants school, exercise equipment, a weekly walk in town when the children could look and learn, a salary (£5 p.a.) for the infants' teacher were some of the subjects on which Mary Ann, on behalf of the Ladies Committee, addressed the gentlemen.

In 1847 she helped found the Ladies Industrial School for the Relief of Irish Destitution caused by the Potato Famine and became its president. Other interests were the Society for the Relief of the Destitute Sick and the Belfast Ladies Clothing Society.

Apsley Place, Donegall Pass

Traffic and shopping once summed up Bradbury Place. Today the traffic shows no sign of decreasing but the shopping outlets have largely been replaced by eateries of various kinds and there is even an hotel.

Some early 19th century houses, once described as 'beautifully situated', survive behind later commercial facades on the left. Lavery's public house occupies a central position. Its mustard coloured facade may not be to everyone's liking but the art nouveau lettering is attractive. This is one of South Belfast's more famous watering holes. In the 1950s it was patronised by sculptor George McCann and his wife whose flat in Botanic Avenue had a private staircase at the rear which gave direct access to Lavery's back door. They brought their friends with them, one of whom was the poet Louis McNeice who featured McCann as Maguire in *Autumn Journal.*

Older folk will remember the Toll House that stood at the junction with Lisburn Road: *"a cosy doll's house of a place"*, Cathal O'Byrne called it. A gate across the road enabled the keeper to collect from traffic entering and leaving the town. The little house seemed to have sunk into the ground but this effect was the result of grading the slope to make it easier for the horse trams. Folklore claims that keeper James Mateer let Queen Victoria through free (he shook her by the hand) but charged her entourage.

Since the Place connects with both the Malone and Lisburn Roads, the old road and the new southwards, it could hardly avoid becoming a traffic bottleneck. A familiar figure in the 1960s was traffic policeman Constable Harry White who did his best to keep motorists and pedestrians happy. His efforts earned him a British Empire Medal and a pile of presents from grateful 'customers' at Christmas.

The towers of the University Road churches provide an inspiring backdrop, lifting the mind, perhaps, to thoughts of fresher air than is obtainable at ground level.

Bradbury Place

The Crescents, Upper or Corry's, 1846, and Lower, 1852, were among the earliest developments above the old shoreline in South Belfast. They were built by Robert Corry, founder of the family firm of J. P. Corry and Co., which was responsible for much mid-19th century building in the University area, including Union Theological College.

Corry's plan was to create the kind of residential arrangement to be found in Dublin, of terraced houses grouped around a central garden. The scheme was not completed since only two terraces were built. Although they are known as the Crescents only one is in fact a crescent. Columns give distinction to the composition of both. Upper Crescent has been described as the *"grandest Neoclassical terrace in Ulster"*.

Robert's home was at number 10 Upper Crescent. A family story relates how he came to live there. He and his wife, Jane, were living in Newtownards where the Corry family had resided for generations. As his business prospered, Robert wished to move to a grander house in Belfast. Jane preferred Newtownards. He set about planning the 'flit'. He invited her to accompany him to Belfast to inspect the company's premises. The day was no doubt to be filled as agreeably as possible, with lunching and shopping included. While the pair were away men cleared The Villa in Church Street, Newtownards, and brought the furniture and fittings to the new house in Corry's Crescent where all was made ready to receive its mistress when she was brought in the evening. Jane accepted her new home and lived out her life there.

The 1850s Crescent residents were chiefly men with town business addresses, among them Robert Boag of the Albion Clothing Company, High Street, and Robert Cassidy, solicitor, Donegall Place. The Crescents were close enough to town to make living over the shop unnecessary. A hundred and fifty years later the pattern is very different. The Crescents are no longer residential and office workers look out over the little park between them.

Mrs Margaret Byers brought her Ladies Collegiate School to a new building at the end of Lower Crescent in 1874 where, renamed Victoria College, it remained until 1972.

The Crescents

Belfast was chosen as the location for one of Sir Robert Peel's Irish colleges. The proposal that the Academical Institution, which already had a collegiate department, should be extended to house the new college was rejected on grounds of expense and a site, ten acres, rural and undeveloped, near the Botanic Gardens was chosen instead. Built to a design by Charles Lanyon which owed its inspiration in part to Magdalene College, Oxford, the College was inaugurated in December 1849 after an inspection by Queen Victoria and Prince Albert a few months earlier.

The College's first President was the Rev. Dr Pooley Shuldham Henry, a Presbyterian minister with a reputation as an organiser. Vice President Dr Thomas Andrews had qualified as a physician before turning to Chemistry, of which subject he was the College's first professor. His work on the liquefaction of gases contributed to the invention of the refrigerator.

A boundary extension report of 1852-3 noted that *"around Queen's College and Botanic Gardens new houses and streets of the best description are fast growing"*. Today University Road is part of a conservation area and many of the mid-Victorian terraces and streets erected in the vicinity of the College (University from 1908) are still standing or have been largely rebuilt. University Square (mainly 1840s), once the grandest address, no longer offers the private residency for which the houses were designed. After a period when it was greatly favoured by the medical profession, it is now in University ownership and the houses accommodate academic departments. A sad loss to the area – suffered in less conservationist times – was brought about by the demolition of Queen's Elms, a Jacobethan terrace across the Road from Lanyon's building, and contemporary with it, to provide a site for a new Students' Union. Dutch Elm Disease, alas, claimed the trees which had given the terrace its name.

The lawns and flowerbeds in front of the old building lend a welcome spaciousness to this stretch of University Road. Letters to successive Vice Chancellors from residents of the area and passers-by have registered public reaction to the way in which this space is used.

University Road

A small group of businessmen and clergy which met in the University area in 1858 was responsible for establishing Elmwood Presbyterian Church. Robert Corry, timber merchant and shipowner, was one the first members of the congregation, contributing generously to the building fund. The church, designed in 'Lombardo-Venetian' style by another member of the Corry family, John, an amateur architect, was built 1859-62. The triple-tiered tower was erected by his family in memory of Robert Corry.

Middle class congregations like Elmwood did not limit their efforts to the spiritual welfare of their own flock, especially when there was an ever growing working class population close by. From the 1870s the Blackstaff (now Donegall) Road was being built on: streets and streets were filling up with unchurched folk. Elmwood established a school on the Blackstaff Road, then a hall/mission, and finally a church, Richview. St. Thomas' on the Lisburn Road contributed to the development of St. Aidan's parish in Sandy Row.

Church work was not limited to saving souls. Individual clergymen, as well as congregations, sought to improve morally and materially the lot of their less fortunate fellows. One such was the Rev. John Edgar who assisted in the formation of the Elmwood congregation. He founded the Presbyterian Orphan Society and the Ulster Female Penitentiary, later known as the Edgar Home, for the rehabilitation of prostitutes, and was involved in setting up the Deaf, Dumb and Blind Institution.

A 20th century member of Elmwood was R. M. Henry, Professor of Latin at Queen's and brother of the painter, Paul Henry. A minister of the church noted wryly that the preacher needed to keep an eye on the Professor because when his head drooped and his pincenez spectacles fell from his nose it was time for the sermon to be wound up.

The Elmwood congregation has joined Fitzroy and the building was sold to the University. Restored and given new windows, it is now home to the Ulster Orchestra.

Elmwood Hall

The Belfast Botanical and Horticultural Society established the Gardens on its present site in 1829. The Society was a private company and an admission charge was levied. In the course of the 19th century the gardens witnessed many interesting events.

Queen Victoria and Prince Albert were shown round by Daniel Ferguson, the curator, during the Queen's only visit to Belfast, in August 1849. A special *"phaeton, lined with purple velvet and painted dark blue, the metalwork silvered, the royal arms on the doors, and drawn by two white ponies"* had been made ready by Belfast coachbuilder William Bathurst to convey the couple through the grounds. But although they admired the vehicle they preferred to stay in their landau. The Queen declared herself *"much pleased"* with what she saw.

Balloon ascents were a popular form of entertainment. In 1864 eleven people ascended in Mr Coswell's 100 feet high balloon 'Britannia', the largest in the world at that time. Thousands filled the gardens in 1867 to witness an ascent by William Hodsman, the first man to cross the Irish Sea by air. When, after six hours, the balloon was still not inflated, a restive crowd had to be bought off with a fireworks display.

A 'spectacular' took place on September 1st, 1885 – a *"Grand Evening Fête when the entire Gardens and shrubberies* (were) *brilliantly illuminated with upwards of 20,000 crystal lamps. Producing a fairy-like effect."* At dusk there were fireworks *"eclipsing any previous pyrotechnic exhibition"* in Belfast, terminating in *"The Storming of Pekin"*. In addition there was a 'Grand Musical Promenade' by the band of the Royal Inniskillings. A lady parachutist drew a crowd in 1891.

On quieter days a visit might be enlivened by a tour of the Palm House, an early example of a curvilinear glass and iron structure, or the Tropical Ravine House, or the Exhibition Hall where dancing was an attraction.

The Gardens were purchased by the City in 1895 for £10,500 and opened as a public park.

Botanic Gardens

"The College occupies an elevated and salubrious site, within an easy distance of the town, and in the immediate vicinity of the Queen's College and Botanic Gardens." (Prospectus 1868)

William Fogarty of Limerick won the competition to design the new Wesleyan Methodist College. The school's church connections probably made a Gothic style the inevitable choice. The new College was to serve a dual function, grammar school and theological college preparing men for the Methodist ministry. Day boys and boarders were catered for. A 15 acre site had been obtained from Miss Harrison of Vermont, Malone Road. Six acres were to accommodate the school while the rest would be let for house-building to provide income.

The theological students were to be housed in single rooms, the schoolboys in dormitories, in two of which each boy would have his own cubicle *so as to secure to a great extent the privacy and comfort of a separate room.* Modern health and safety experts will note with approval the provision of WCs, baths, hot and cold water, and a stone staircase as a safeguard against fire. Two physicians were appointed to attend the sick in the school infirmary.

On offer was 'an unbroken course' from preparatory department to graduation from university. A kindergarten was opened; girls were admitted from 1869. Hours were 10am to 3pm, except on Saturdays when school got out

at noon. Indiscipline was punished by extra work and detention; incorrigibles were asked to leave. The sexes were segregated and even outside school boys seen talking to girls might be reprimanded.

The College grew rapidly. Fortunately the governors did not yield to the temptation to raise money by letting more land, so that space was available for extensions, for example McArthur Hall, accommodation for female boarders.

Among the thousands of alumni who have enriched our society are Robert Graecen, poet and critic, Patric Stevenson, artist, John D. Stewart, broadcaster, John E. Sayers, editor-in-chief, Belfast Telegraph, Barry Douglas, pianist and Ernest Walton, Nobel Prize for Physics (1951).

Methodist College: McArthur Hall

The 'mother church' of Roman Catholicism in South Belfast is St. Malachy's in the Markets area, close to the old town centre. When the suburbs began to blossom the Church turned its attention to the need for new accommodation there. Two churches were built in South Belfast, St. Brigid's and the Holy Rosary.

The former owes its origin in part to the fact that the big houses in Malone were largely staffed by Roman Catholic servants. They found St. Malachy's too distant and asked for a more convenient place of worship. Bishop McAllister was sympathetic, land was leased and a church in vaguely Italian-Romanesque style consecrated in 1893. The Holy Rosary on the Ormeau Road opened in 1898.

Both buildings have been superseded: St. Brigid's by a new church on the Malone Road; the Rosary has been closed and the congregation now worships in the former convent chapel opposite (Church of the Good Shepherd). A competition to find a design for the new St. Brigid's was won by Messrs Kennedy, Fitzgerald and Associates. The judges, in commending the design, noted:– *"fundamentally the building was ... most elegantly detailed (and coloured), clearly a calm and comfortable place to be, with the roof forming a uniting canopy above both ministers and congregation ... mortuary, baptistry, stairs, entrances, sanctuary are allowed to grow naturally out from under it to make a well-balanced composition of both general and particular space."*

The spirit that inspired Protestants at the end of the 18th century to contribute to the cost of building the first Roman Catholic church in Belfast, St. Mary's, was again in evidence when local congregations offered gifts to the new St. Brigid's.

The most adventurous Roman Catholic church in South Belfast architecturally is St. Bernadette's on the Upper Knockbreda Road (1966). The fan-shaped brick and reinforced concrete building is lit by large expanses of coloured glass; a bronze figure of Christ by Elizabeth Frink hangs above the altar.

St. Brigid's, Malone Road

Fortunes made in town businesses, ship-building, linen, engineering, banking and commerce paid for new residences for the upper classes who were deserting the increasingly unfashionable neighbourhood of Donegall Place from the mid 19th century. Batts built at Purdysburn; others found sites on the Malone ridge.

The linen industry was well represented there. Samuel Barbour (linen thread) employed W. J. Barre, of Albert Clock fame, to build the palatial Danesfort, a house combining English, French and Italian elements in its design. The most striking feature is the tower which accommodated 'retiring rooms'. Richardsons lived at Brooklands on the Lisburn Road, James Ward of the Belfast Linen and Damask Co., at Cherry Hill and Robert Lindsay at Sans Souci.

Fortunes from tea set up Forster Green at Derryvolgie and Thomas Johnston, great-grandfather of the novelist Jennifer Johnston, at Dunarnon. The wholesale drinks trade provided for Robert Atkinson at Beaumont. Atkinson invested some of the profits in house-building on the Malone Road and was a generous benefactor to several churches, donating stained glass windows (Knockbreda) and a peal of bells (St. Thomas'). Another wholesale wines and spirits merchant to achieve Malone Road status was William Greer of Kirker, Greer and Co., who was to be found living at Danesfort in 1900.

The engineering family of Musgrave, four bachelor brothers, built Drumglass. They gave part of the grounds to the City for a public park in 1924. Members of the Corry family, timber merchants, builders and ship-owners, built Dunraven and Benvue.

Walter H. Wilson (family home Maryville) of Harland & Wolff preferred to rent. He leased Stranmillis House, which was excellent for the entertaining he loved, much of it connected with customers of the shipyard. However it did not provide the game shooting he craved and he gave up Stranmillis for Belvoir Park where he was able to indulge in serious country sports.

Some of these grand houses have survived though put to other uses, for example, Drumglass now belongs to Victoria College and Danesfort is offices. The little demesnes have been built over.

Danesfort

Cranmore, Malone, has played a modest role in Irish history at both ends of the political spectrum. In June 1690 William III began a march from Belfast that would bring him to victory at the battle of the Boyne. His route took him southwards along the Malone ridge. Rain was falling as he and his men were passing Cranmore and the owner, a Mr Eccles, invited the King to shelter in his house. In honour of the occasion Eccles called his home Orange Grove.

A hundred years later Orange Grove was home to a man with rather different political views, John Templeton. Though tempting offers were made to him to settle in Australia he preferred to devote his talents to the study of Irish flora, becoming an accomplished plant illustrator in the process. His political opinions were expressed in his membership of the Society of United Irishmen (he joined in 1797 but did not take part in the '98 Rebellion) and in his friendship with Linen Hall librarian Thomas Russell, 'the man from God knows where'. Russell joined Templeton in long walks in the Ulster countryside: walks which Templeton remembered with pleasure in letters to Russell languishing in Kilmainham Gaol. Dr James McDonnell made a third in these rambles, but the relationship between him and Templeton cooled when McDonnell was persuaded to contribute to a fund offered for information that would lead to Russell's arrest following the failure of Robert Emmet's plot to capture Dublin Castle, for which he had tried to drum up support.

Russell was hanged in Downpatrick in 1803. Mrs McTier wrote to her brother, Dr Drennan, *"I hear J. Templeton has withdrawn from the L(iterary) Society to avoid his former friend, McD."* A reconciliation between the two men was effected by Templeton's sister shortly before his death.

Templeton compiled a catalogue of native plants but died before he finished his Flora Hibernica. He made a further contribution to learning in Ulster through his involvement in the establishment of Belfast 'Inst.' whose playing fields neighbour the ruin of his home.

Ruin of Cranmore, Malone

William Wallace inherited the Legg estate at Malone in 1821 on the death of his uncle. He added Legge to his surname (and the final e). He built the present house, the third on the site since the 17th century, and may have been his own architect. The principal rooms were arranged to provide splendid views across the Lagan valley and he moved the public road in order to improve the approach to his house. Being High Sheriff probably made it easier for him to do so. He planted many trees and managed to obtain outright ownership of the land, hitherto held on a series of leases, from the Donegall family.

A late marriage to an English heiress produced a son and a daughter. The son proved a disappointment, squandering money and getting deeply into debt. Perhaps his family was relieved when he sold his interest in the estate to his father and departed for America. He then moved to Australia where his first wife was murdered in Adelaide. There were two more marriages before he drank himself to death.

William's daughter, Florence, did rather better, though certain aspects of her behaviour would have raised eyebrows in the upper class circles of the time. She supported votes for women and enjoyed cycling, wearing the garment of the emancipated woman, bloomers. She married the heir of Viscount Harberton. At her own request her funeral was the cheapest possible.

After W. W. Legge's death in 1868 the estate was let to tenants. In 1920 the house and some of the land were bought by J.M.K. McGugan, an insurance broker who had made a fortune in Mexican Eagle oil shares. His investment in Harper Beans, however, collapsed and he was forced to sell the following year.

The new owner was William Barnett whose horse Trigo won both the Derby and the St Leger in 1929. The last private owner, he left the house and grounds to Belfast for use as a public park.

Destroyed by an IRA bomb in 1976, the house was splendidly rebuilt under the direction of architects McKinstry and Brown.

Malone House

Shaw's Bridge has long been a popular spot with walkers on the Lagan towpath. A Colonel Brown reported from Belfast, 13 June , 1655: *"Att the Lagan near the fort of Hilsbowre in Mylone* (Malone) *Captt. Shaw of ye train has layed a bridge of bawk* (bog) *oak timbre and pales. A platform of oak spares over which gun carriages have been the first to pass this daye"*. Shaw was an artillery officer in Cromwell's army and the site he chose for his bridge had probably been an ancient crossing point. An old name for the crossing was *Athmagh-luan*, the ford of the plain of the lambs. The first stone bridge, built in 1698, was destroyed by a flood in 1709. According to tradition materials from a ruin on the hill above the river, Castle Cam, were used in the rebuilding.

The Lagan canal was constructed between Belfast and Lisburn 1754-63 and extended to Lough Neagh by 1793, the Earl of Donegall contributing £60,000 to complete the latter section.

The Navigation was inaugurated by Belfast merchant Thomas Greg in September 1763 when he, his wife, a select party of friends and a band travelled on the lighter 'Lord Hertford' from Belfast to Lisburn. A crowd of several hundred followed on the towpath. Refreshments were served on board.

Greg had a particular interest in the Lagan Navigation. He and his brother-in-law, Waddell Cunningham, established a vitriol (sulphuric acid) works at Lisburn.

Vitriol reduced the time required to bleach brown linen from days to hours. The lighters carried the raw materials to Lisburn and brought the dangerous finished product to Belfast.

An interesting cargo that made the journey all the way from Lough Neagh to Belfast can still be seen in High Street, the portico of St. George's Church, once the entrance front of Ballyscullion House, county Londonderry, a property of Frederick Hervey, the Earl-Bishop.

The Lagan Navigation ceased to operate in the 1950s: the M1 now covers part of it.

Increasing traffic made the old bridge a bottleneck and a new, single-span structure a little way downstream was opened in 1976.

Shaw's Bridge & Lagan Towpath

A church at Drum is recorded in the ecclesiastical taxation roll of 1306. A new building replaced an older one in 1798. The tower is the chief survival of 18th century St Patrick's; the spire was rebuilt in 1833 and the main body 1868-1870. The distinguishing mark of the churchyard is the lych gate given by Ellen Caldwell in memory of her brother John Montgomery of Ballydrain in 1878.

An interesting story attaches to the grave in the churchyard of James Haddock, *"who dweled in Mallon"* and who died in 1657. Five years later Francis Taverner was confronted at Drumbridge by Haddock's ghost and urged to obtain justice for Haddock's son who, it was alleged, had been cheated by his stepfather over a lease. Taverner's reluctance to carry out the spirit-given charge led, according to the report drawn up for Bishop Jeremy Taylor, to much suffering for him through further ghostly visitations. The case was eventuallty settled in favour of Haddock's son. One version of the story has the ghost making an appearance in court. The jury declared itself convinced by this evidence from beyond the grave.

Many members of South Belfast gentry and commercial families are buried in the churchyard and it is said to contain the graves of Protestants massacred in the 1641 Rebellion. More recently interred were William Wallace Legge, builder of Malone House, and Patricia Curran, the twenty-year old daughter of Lord Justice Curran, whose murder caused a sensation in 1952.

The bridge at Drum was built sometime before 1750. The lock near Drumbridge was the sixth of 17 leading to the head level of the Lagan Navigation. The stretch of waterway at Ballydrain had a reputation for spookiness (including an apparition of a headless horseman) and superstitious lightermen hurried past to Drum. The river between Lambeg and Drum is celebrated in the romantic song *'My Lagan Love'*, about the bargeman's daughter who had the poet's:–

"heart in thrall
Nor life I owe, nor liberty,
For Love is Lord of all."

St. Patrick's Church, Drumbeg

Post-war expansion of university education brought a need for more accommodation at Queen's. In his history of the University, Professor J. C. Beckett remarked that between the late 1940s and the early 1980s there was hardly a year when a new building scheme was not occupying the University's planners. The old College site on University Road could not provide space for all that was required. Vice Chancellor David Keir obtained a large site between the Malone and Stranmillis Roads on which the Keir and Ashby buildings were to be erected. The arrival of these colossi seriously disturbed the domestic scale of the area.

Houses on both roads, which included Eisleben House at the corner of Chlorine Gardens, were cleared away in preparation for building. The existence of a former sandpit explains why the Ashby car park is so far below road level. The Keir was designed with its main entrance facing townwards since the original intention was to buy up and demolish the houses in the angle between the two roads. But house prices made purchase impossible and so side doors have had to be used instead.

Engineering, formerly taught at the College of Technology, Chemistry and Biological Sciences were relocated in the brick, neo-Georgian, Keir building, which was opened by the Duke of Edinburgh in 1959. The tower-block Ashby Institute joined the Keir in 1965 (Electrical and Mechanical Engineering). When former Vice Chancellor, Lord Ashby of Brandon, after whom the building is named, opened the Institute in 1965 he took great pleasure in the fact that the loo paper was embossed 'Ashby'. Student humour in higher echelons?

By that time construction on the site had been going on for 15 years. When work was completed the University gave a party for the residents of the area who, no doubt, were happy to help celebrate the departure of the builders.

Major building projects were also carried out on the old College site (Physics, library and administration), Elmwood Avenue (Geology) and Lisburn Road (Medical Biology Centre).

Stranmillis Road

The first provincial museum in Ireland erected by voluntary subscription was opened in 1831 in College Square North by the Belfast Natural History and Philosophical Society. Transferred to the Belfast Corporation in 1910, the collections found an honoured place at Stranmillis when the new Museum opened in 1929.

Generations of Belfast children -- and their parents -- have gazed fascinated at Takabuti, the Egyptian mummy whose coffin was brought to the Old Museum in 1835 and the inscriptions explained by Egyptologist and Assyriologist, the Rev. Dr Edward Hincks, rector of Killyleagh.

Another interesting item is the Solomon Islands canoe, 39 feet long, 3 feet 6 inches in beam, made from planks chopped into shape by stone hatchets and stitched together with split rattan covered with native gum. It made its last head-hunting expedition in 1896.

Henry Joy McCracken and other men of '98 have a display to themselves which includes McCracken's coat and sword worn at the battle of Antrim. The Museum also has the roughly hewn, white sandstone state chair of the O'Neills of Clannaboy.

A notable addition to the collections is material from the 'Girona', a ship of the Spanish Armada wrecked off the Antrim coast in 1588. The most touching item is a ring showing a heart held by a hand and a buckle and inscribed with the words 'No tengo mas que dar te' (I have nothing more to give you).

New approaches to display have revolutionised the presentation of antiquities. Visitors can make a journey from pre-historic times to the Early Christian period, passing reconstructions of dwellings and scenes from everyday life. There are opportunities for hands-on involvement. The dinosaurs gallery is a certain success with youngsters addicted to films of the 'Jurassic Park' genre.

Irish artists Nicholl, Lavery, Conor, O'Connor, Flannigan, Middleton, etc., are well represented in the art gallery on the upper floor. Acquisitions have not always been made peacefully. A proposal to purchase a picture by William Scott in the 1950s showed some members of the Belfast Corporation's Museum Committee to be seriously out of touch with modern art.

The building was extended 1963-71.

The Ulster Museum

Richard Hayward attributed to Friar's Bush a *"quality of ancient mystery"*. But how ancient? A Patrician foundation as some have suggested? The stone inscribed *'This stone marks ye friar's grave AD 485'* may be dismissed as romantic nonsense. The site, without a church, is marked on a map of 1570. The picture becomes clearer when we reach the penal times (in Irish *An Drocht Shaol)* of the 18th century. Forbidden to build a church in town or to conduct worship in public, Catholics met at Friar's Bush, outside the town boundary, to receive Holy Communion at an altar placed in the shelter of a thorn. The bush survives. Mass ceased to be celebrated at Friar's Bush in 1769 when the relaxing of the penal laws enabled premises to be leased in Mill (now Castle) Street. The graveyard became the chief burial place for Catholics until the opening of Milltown Cemetery in 1869, by which time there was no more burial space in Friar's Bush.

In the 19th century the graveyard acquired a more sinister character. The unhealthy town of Belfast was subject to epidemics. Cholera in 1832-3 sent more than four hundred for burial in a fever pit at Friar's Bush. In 1847, during the Famine, they were joined by victims of typhus. It has been estimated that the remains of twelve hundred people lie under The 'Plaguey Hill', the nickname for the mound on the north side of the cemetery.

Though the names of the plague victims are not carved on any stones, memorials of various kinds record the names of distinguished members of the Catholic community buried here. These include three newspapermen, Kevin T. Buggy (his memorial was 'Erected by the Repealers of Belfast'), Robert Read and A. J. McKenna. Read established Belfast's first penny newspaper, 'The Belfast Morning News'; it merged with the 'Irish News' in 1891. Bernard Hughes, who arrived penniless in Belfast from County Armagh, built up one of Ireland's biggest bakeries and became the town's first Catholic alderman, also lies here with his two wives and several of his children.

Friar's Bush Cemetery

In 1922 the new Northern Ireland government acquired 46 acres at Stranmillis, once part of Lady Donegall's 'very fine park', on which to build a teacher-training college. Hitherto student-teachers had finished their training in Dublin.

In the early days, since the College had no buildings of its own, practical classes were taught in Belfast 'Tech' and academic subjects at Queen's University. The first principal was W. J. McCallister, Professor of Education at Queen's. The neo-Georgian College building was officially opened on 1st May, 1930, an occasion described in the press as 'very jolly'.

Women students were accommodated in 'Bungalow Hostels' and in Stranmillis House, built 1857-8 by Messrs Lanyon and Lynn for Thomas G. Batt, a director of the Belfast Bank, which was adapted for the purpose. House rules for the women were strict, regulating meal times, tidiness of bedrooms and reception of visitors (in common rooms only and not after 5.15pm). Students had to be in College by 6.15pm except on Saturday and Sunday when they were allowed out to 10 pm. Lights out 10.45pm. Lights left burning in bedrooms during daytime meant a 6d fine.

Residential accommodation kept the sexes rigorously apart. Hampton House, the former Girls Industrial School in Balmoral Avenue, renamed Balmoral Hall, was the men's hostel. It was inconveniently located since there was no public transport from it to the College. Walking or cycling to Stranmillis no doubt kept the men fit. The segregation of the sexes was reflected in the College building by separate entrances and staircases for men and women students.

During the 1926-7 session Stranmillis Public Elementary School was transferred to the College for demonstration purposes and a gallery installed so that students could watch lessons being taught.

The post-war demand for teachers caused a rise in student numbers and more accommodation was required. The Orchard Building was erected 1952-3. Major development from the 1960s provided halls of residence, the Central Building (housing the main teaching block and library), a theatre and the circular Music Department.

Stranmillis is now fully integrated into Queen's University.

Stranmillis College

A '90s development on the Lagan at Stranmillis is Cutters Wharf, a pub-restaurant designed, reputedly, in the guise of a dock-side warehouse. This is not the first such establishment at this point on the river.

Nearby in the late 18th century was to be found Molly Ward's tavern, a fashionable spot apparently, where patrons might enjoy the garden and drink ales and spirits or spoon *"cruds and cream"*. It was probably its location well away from the town that made it popular with members of the Society of United Irishmen in the 1790s. Arms and ammunition could be smuggled up river to Ward's prior to distribution in County Down.

On one occasion it seems that there was only time to dump the arms into the river before the soldiers were banging on the door. (A vengeful employee of the Stranmillis Calico Works has been accused of spilling the beans.) Unfortunately a keg of gunpowder had been overlooked in the rush to clear the evidence of rebellious intent. Molly covered it with clothes, set her elderly mother-in-law on top and gave her the baby to hold, hoping the soldiers would not be too curious in that direction. She kept up a flow of chatter and even showed them the ancient gun kept to protect the lock. She got away with it.

The original Molly Ward's island hostelry is long gone, as is another establishment of the same name which featured for a time on the 'mainland'. The site of the former is presently occupied by the Belfast Boat Club, formed by a coming together of the Ulster Athletic and Rowing Club and the Lagan Amateur Rowing Club. Mrs W. J. Pirrie, wife of the Harland and Wolff chief, declared the Club House open in 1898. Until the lock was filled in access was by punt. A 50lb terrorist bomb wrecked the building, including the new bar and lounge, in 1972. A phoenix arose from the ashes in the form of a new, top-of-the-range complex. Oddly enough the Boat Club does not row: its interest is tennis.

Cutters Wharf

The City Hospital occupies the site of the Belfast Union Workhouse set up under the Irish Poor Relief Act of 1838. The Belfast Board of Guardians acquired a 12 acre site between the Lisburn and Donegall Roads and opened the Workhouse in 1841. The Union stretched to Greencastle on one side of Belfast Lough and to Holywood on the other.

Belfast's workhouse, built in a Tudor-Jacobean style, was one of the largest and, reputedly, one of the best equipped in Ireland. The Irish Poor Law Commissioners stated, *"The style of building is intended to be of the cheapest description compatible with durability; and effect is aimed at by harmony of proportion and simplicity of arrangement, all mere decoration being studiously excluded."* Interior walls were whitewashed, roof timbers left exposed. Inmates slept on straw mattresses laid out on sleeping platforms. Discipline was strict; offending adults could be locked up or excluded and boys whipped. Diet was described as monotonous and poor. Official policy was that Workhouse food *"must on no account be superior or even equal to the ordinary mode of subsistence of the labouring classes"* (cynics suggested that this was impossible!). Those entering surrendered their clothes, were fumigated, and given a uniform. Not the least, perhaps, of the pains of entering the Workhouse was the splitting up of families inside it.

Authority was represented by the Master and the Matron. The first Master, Arthur Connor, and his wife (Matron) were sacked and the latter also fined when she was found guilty of striking the Workhouse schoolteacher, Mrs Evans. Connor was accused of intimidating pauper witnesses, who were only persuaded to testify against his wife when given police protection.

A hundred years after the Connor affair, in 1939, another Master was dismissed and the Board dissolved when an enquiry revealed mismanagement. Two government appointees took charge.

The windows of the new tower-block City Hospital offer prospects brighter, literally and metaphorically, than did those of the older establishment.

City Hospital

Second Belfast (Presbyterian), formed in 1708, worshipped in a building in Rosemary Street. The congregation, adhering to the New Light side of the 18th century controversy that divided Presbyterians, set an example of tolerance by insisting on the right of private judgment in matters theological. Subscription to the Westminster Confession of Faith was not required of its members.

A significant event in the church's history was the installation of an organ in 1806, a major departure for a dissenting congregation, the only other church in Belfast with an organ being St Anne's. The first organist was Edward Bunting of Belfast Harp Festival fame. Boys for the choir were found in the Poor House. They were allowed a guinea a year *"as an encouragement to learn"*.

From mid-century the character of the town centre had been changing, residents were moving out, many of them to South Belfast, commerce moving in. In 1893 the minister of Second Belfast, the Rev. E. I. Fripp, told his flock that if their congregation was *"to have a new lease of life"*, they must leave Rosemary Street.

The people agreed, the Rosemary Street building was sold and a church built on suburban Elmwood Avenue. The building, in late 14th century Gothic style, would not look out of place in an English village but demand for building sites in the Avenue has denied it its village green and churchyard. The lack of divisions, screens, a communion rail, in the internal arrangements, according to S. S. Millin, reflects the spirit of freedom valued by the congregation throughout its long history. Inscribed on the porch are the words 'All Souls Are Mine', hence the name by which the church is known.

Second Belfast was not the only congregation to react to changing patterns by moving to the suburbs. Alfred Street Presbyterian sold up in 1872 and opened a new church in the then suburban Fitzroy Avenue (now University Street). Fisherwick vacated College Square East and relocated on Malone Road.

All Souls Church, Elmwood Avenue

The 'wee shop' from which 'My Aunt Jane' gave me 'three black lumps' probably no longer exists, though practically every street corner in the blue collar areas of South Belfast once had one. 'Open all hours', they personified convenience shopping. Places where one might get credit from a shop keeper who was at the same time a neighbour.

The main roads, with two notable exceptions, had their shopping 'centres' at intervals along the way. The exceptions were, and are, Malone and Ravenhill, (Malone telephoned and the goods were delivered!). While these centres remain, though new types of trading have in many cases replaced the old, the arrival of the mall and supermarket (see Forestside) has brought changes in shopping habits and in the relationship betweeen customer and supplier. Population shift has had its effect too: Shaftesbury Square-Bradbury Place-Donegall Pass, which once made a wide area of South Belfast practically self-sufficient, is no longer a shopping centre.

Memories of the old days linger.

A major outlet on the Ormeau Road, once, was Downings' hardware store. Former Ballynafeigh resident Roy Allen remembers it with affection:–

"The ground floor contained every conceivable item of hardware and ironmongery … newspapers, magazine and comics … various types of oil (were sold) … acid batteries for the wireless were recharged … hurricane lamps, tools of all descriptions … iron griddles … walking sticks and canes … including whipping canes with round handles … for administering swift justice to mischievous children. On the first floor were all types of delph and china … The floor above housed Adam Turner, complete funeral furnisher."

Further down the Ormeau Road was Linton's second hand furniture and junk shop, on a site now occupied by Havelock House. Of special interest among his stock was old cine film which he sold by the yard to small boys who made it into 'smoke bombs'.

In Cromac Street James Lundy presided over an emporium which boasted of selling everything from a donkey to a four-engined bomber. One can only speculate what the delivery time was on the latter.

And with what pleasure one entered Marshall's grocery shop on Botanic Avenue with all its tempting aromas.

Shopping: Lisburn Road

The North Eastern Agricultural Association – predecessor of the R.U.A.S. – held its first annual Show at the Balmoral premises in 1896. Prize money amounted to £1,000 and there were 1,391 entries. The Show was suspended during the two World Wars when the grounds and buildings were put to other uses. Intimidation during the Ulster Workers Strike forced a last minute postponement in May 1974 and the 'troubles' reduced attendances from across the border.

The showgrounds have hosted events other than agricultural. In 1912 airman H. J. D. Astley was killed there when the Bleriot monoplane in which he was giving a flying display crashed. The incident is believed to have been the first aviation accident in Ireland.

Politics have also featured. On Easter Tuesday 1912 some one hundred thousand people gathered at Balmoral to declare their opposition to Home Rule, bringing with them a Union Jack measuring 48 feet by 25, reputedly the largest in the world. Conservative party leader Andrew Bonar Law told the crowd *"You are a besieged city. The timid have left you; your Lundies have betrayed you; but you have closed your gates."* A rally of similar proportions in 1962, and featuring the same flag, commemorated the fiftieth anniversary of the signing of the Ulster Covenant.

The principal building on the site, called the King's Hall after George V, opened in May 1934. It was intended to be Belfast's Olympia. As such it has hosted Ideal Home Exhibitions, religious revival campaigns, pop concerts and boxing matches. Rinty Monaghan took the World Flyweight Championship from Jackie Patterson in the Hall in 1948 and Barry McGuiggan fought there in the 1980s.

Controversy surrounded a fight in 1935 when local hero Jimmy Warnock was floored by Frenchman Maurice Huguenin in the second round. Consternation among Warnock's fans! The referee had reached a count of seven when someone saved the day by plunging the hall in darkness. When the lights came on again Warnock was being attended to in his corner. He went on to win.

A visit to the 2002 Show was part of the Queen's Golden Jubilee progamme in Northern Ireland.

Royal Ulster Agricultural Society

The white neo-Georgian Christian Science complex on University Avenue was begun in 1923 with the building of the school; a minister's house followed in 1928; the church was erected 1936-7 and dedicated, 'free of debt', in 1944. The architect was Clough Williams-Ellis, the creator of Portmeirion in Wales.

A walk in South Belfast, especially in the University area, will reveal considerable variety in church architecture.

Until about the 1860s the Presbyterians preferred the Classical style, leaving Gothic to the Anglicans and Roman Catholics. Perhaps it was a way of expressing theological difference: not for them pre-Reformation pointed arches and dim religious light filtered through stained glass. After 1870 Gothic was adopted, sometimes with really interesting results, witness the belfry of Crescent Church. Gothic Fitzroy, Fisherwick and Newtownbreda each replaced a classical building. Elmwood has a good claim to be the most exotic Presbyterian church built in south Belfast. The carved decoration is well worth a closer look, especially the loggia capitals (plant studies), work attributed to the highly talented Fitzpatricks whose sculptures adorn McCausland's warehouse in Victoria Street and the Custom House.

The Methodists on the lower Ormeau Road and on University Road opted for designs inspired by northern Italy before they really went over the top at Ballynafeigh with a church described at the time as in 'American-Byzantine' style. It is less spiky in appearance today because spire, fleche and finials have been removed. The galleried interior resembles an Elizabethan theatre.

The Church of Ireland settled for Gothic, Early English being most commonly used. 'Old' St. John's, Malone, was the first. When the Classical St. Mary Magdalene on Donegall Pass was destroyed by fire its successor was a Gothic building.

The stained glass in many of the churches originated from the firm of Meyer of Munich and is rarely exciting. A church to benefit from the 20th century Irish renaissance in stained glass was St. John's, Malone, which has notable windows by internationally acclaimed designers Evie Hone and Wilhemina Geddes.

First Church of Christ Scientist

Two hundred years ago Ireland had one university, Trinity College, Dublin; Scotland with a much smaller population had five. Trinity was a Church of Ireland stronghold: Presbyterians had actually been excluded until 1793. Candidates for the Presbyterian ministry studied at Scottish universities, Glasgow being the most popular. The student setting off to college with his sack of meal was once a powerful image for Ulster Presbyterians.

Ulster's need for a college of higher education seemed met with the opening of the Belfast Academical Institution in 1814 with a collegiate department where ministerial candidates were taught. Unfortunately 'Inst.' became caught up in theological controversy.

The issue dividing Presbyterians was subscription to the Westminster Confession of Faith. The leading figures in the debate were Dr Henry Cooke, minister of May Street Presbyterian Church, the champion of orthodoxy, and Dr Henry Montgomery of Dunmurry. The Church split; congregations refusing to subscribe formed the Remonstrant Synod. The rest accepted obligatory subscription and joined with the Seceders to form the General Assembly in 1840. Some of the Remonstrant ministers openly declared their Arianism, the denial of the full divinity of Christ. Cooke and his supporters saw too much Arian influence in 'Inst.' (is that why his statue stands with its back to it?) and set about establishing a theological college that would be under General Assembly control.

The government refused to grant-aid a 'sectarian' college. The Presbyterians went ahead independently and their college, for long known as Assembly's, opened in December 1853 (architect Charles Lanyon). Cooke, who had been rejected as President of Queen's, having been described by the Home Secretary as *"a violent, headstrong man unable to control himself and not likely to command others by conciliatory means"*, was its first president and Professor of Sacred Rhetoric and Catechetics.

Controversy again divided the Presbyterian Church in the 1920s, when College Professor Ernest Davey was charged with teaching heresy. Unable to accept his acquittal by a Church court Davey's accusers withdrew to form the Irish Evangelical Church.

Now a recognised college of Queen's University 'Assembly's' has been linked with Methodist Edgehill and renamed Union Theological College.

Union Theological College

Cave Hill and McArt's Fort provide a splendid backdrop to the lower Ormeau Road. This section of the Road originated as one of the 3rd Earl of Donegall's passages, or passes, cut through the Cromac Woods at the end of the 17th century, and known as Long Pass. Housing development (terraces) began in the 1830s. One of the early residents was 19th century Presbyterian Belfast's 'pope', Dr Henry Cooke of May Street Church.

The Gasworks was opened in 1823 by a private company to provide the town with street lighting:– *"the said gaslight to be equal to that supplied to the public lamps in London and to be three times greater in brightness than the oil light now existing in said town of Belfast"*. According to the News Letter, Belfast was delighted with the new amenity. The 3rd Earl's other improvement, Cromac Dock, enabled barges to unload coal for gas manufacture.

For some considerable time gas was suitable for use only in open thoroughfares or large rooms, being smelly and hot. The invention of the incandescent mantle made gas lighting cheaper and brighter and brought it on to the domestic scene. The coin-in-the-slot metre and the distribution of free light fittings and rings for cooking benefited the poorer classes. Under the management of the Stelfoxes, father and son, the Gasworks grew to cover an area of 23 acres. Some notable interiors were created. The office building has a grand tiled entrance hall and staircase and the middle section meter house had a glazed dome. The pedimented brick retort house with its

splendid Belfast coat-of-arms in sandstone, won the admiration of John Betjeman. Its remoteness from management in the offices further down the road is said to explain its nickname, the Klondyke. Its life as a retort house was short: smoke generated there interfered with linen bleaching nearby and the linen manufacturer won an injunction against the Gasworks.

Belfast Corporation acquired the Gasworks in 1874. Profits subsidised the rates and contributed towards the cost of building the City Hall and the Albert Bridge. Competition from electricity eventually brought closure in 1988.

ORMEAU ROAD

Donegall Pass streets, Oak, Elm, etc., took names suggested by the area over which they were built, the Cromac Woods; an Ormeau Road area did the job in reverse by taking its name, the Holy Land, from the streets: Palestine, Jerusalem, etc.

The Holy Land site was once the Cromac Park estate, land bounded by present day University Street, Ormeau Road and the river, stretching almost to the Presbyterian College on Botanic Avenue. The last resident was James Neill, flour merchant of King Street. A map of about 1870 shows the Park nicely hedged with trees, the middle ground open, and through it flows the Belfast Old Water Course from Stranmillis to the Basin in what is now Ormeau Avenue.

The housing development was hatched apparently by estate agent R. J. McConnell and developer James Rea during a holiday in the Middle East, hence the street names. The houses were superior to the industrial housing closer to town and attracted a more prosperous type of tenant. The proximity of the Botanic Gardens and of the Ormeau Park would have encouraged setting up home in the Holy Land.

When the site was being prepared for building (1892) evidence was found of occupation by an ancient people who used flint tools, cores from which flakes were struck, scrapers, axes, and arrowheads. Similar finds were made over the river where Delhi and Agra Streets were built.

Today many residents find the Holy Land most unholy. Speculators have been buying up houses for letting to students who, the residents believe, are responsible for a rise in the anti-social behaviour in the area which is forcing people out. Young families cannot afford the inflated house prices (small terraced houses can fetch six-figure sums); school enrollment consequently is reduced; older people are adversely affected because traditional support systems are being lost and the community sent into decline. Residents have warned the statutory authorities that something must be done to preserve such traditional communities in South Belfast.

The Holy Land

A minor pleasure to be enjoyed when walking on the Ormeau Road in the vicinity of the Park is the smell of freshly baked bread emanating from Ormeau Bakery.

As Belfast grew in the 19th century so did demands on those 'ministering to food', among whom were numbered the bakers. Robert Wilson learned the business from his older brother John who had a bakery in Great Edward (now Victoria) Street. He opened up on his own account in Cromac Street in 1875, moving the business to its present site, then on the outskirts of the city, in 1890. The bakery prospered and the premises had to be extended four times to cope with increasing demand.

In the early days the bread was distributed by handcarts; expanded trade required horse-drawn vehicles whose animals were stabled nearby. The bakery prided itself on being ahead of its rivals in introducing new equipment and techniques. It was the first to own a fleet of electric vans, 50 of them by 1935.

Three generations of the Wilson family ran the bakery until it was taken over by Andrews Flour Mills in 1980. Mother's Pride N.I. are the present owners.

Is the bakery haunted? There are workers at Ormeau who are prepared to go on record as having seen a spectral visitor on the premises, a 'blue lady', who has appeared during late shifts.

The Belfast directory for 1950 lists 163 names under bakeries, 46 of them in South Belfast. Many were small affairs and they probably mainly sold bread produced by the bigger companies. A personal note was struck by the use of the proprietor's name, for example, Miss Ethel Gray, instead of a trade name. Between the single shop and the 'big boys' were the home bakeries, Whites, etc. Was 'home' meant to imply bread such as mother baked?

Most of these smaller businesses throughout Belfast have been absorbed by the larger concerns. How large might be suggested by the production at Ormeau of three-quarters of a million pancakes for Shrove Tuesday.

Ormeau Bakery

In the 1860s the Good Shepherd Sisters established a refuge for women caught in 'illegitimate pregnancies' or who were anxious to escape from prostitution. Their first house, Bankmore, on Dublin Road, proved unhealthy because of flooding by the nearby Blackstaff and, after an outbreak of fever in which one of the Sisters died, a new location was found on the upper Ormeau Road. A convent, chapel and refuge were built to designs by Alex McAllister. As the work increased new buildings were added. Since the women were expected to contribute to their keep a steam laundry, the first in Belfast, was set up to provide employment.

A new convent chapel (now known as the Church of the Good Shepherd) was built during the Great War. Its Carrara marble main altar survived a bombing attack and a fire on the ship bringing it from Italy.

Catholic social work was further developed in the Ormeau-Ravenhill area with the establishment of Nazareth House for girls and the aged poor, St Joseph's Home for babies and Nazareth Lodge Home for boys. An admission to the last created a sensation in 1956. He was nicknamed the Hen House Boy. Discovered locked in a shed on a farm near Crossgar, the boy, aged between six and seven, was described by a doctor as having *"sharp features, rickety legs and a curved spine, suggestive of habitual roosting, (he) could not speak, but made animal noises which became hen-like when poultry food was provided."* He weighed just 28 pounds (normal weight for his age 50 pounds). The welfare authorities described him as *"a desperate case"* and *"wholly unbelievable."*

A nun recalls him *"responding to love, enjoying music, … requiring a lot of medical treatment … his speech seriously affected"*. He later found sheltered employment with the Sisters of Charity. Seamus Heaney pondered the boy's story in a poem, "Bye-Child".

Nazareth House and the former home of Bishop Dorrian have been demolished to make way for new housing. A new Care Village has been opened on the Ravenhill Road.

Good Shepherd Convent, Ormeau Road

Close to the junction of the Ormeau and Ravenhill Roads is a row of early 19th century cottages known as Saddlers' Row, the oldest houses in the area. Farmers coming into Belfast markets would leave bits of harness, etc. to be repaired at the cottages, collecting them on the way home.

Resident at the Row in the 1930s was Lizzie Moodie, a 'character' whose spring cleaning brought the entire contents of her home, chamber pot included, on to the street so that she could get to work on the interior. She kept a bucket of water behind her front door to empty over anyone who, innocently, offended her by waiting at the tramstop nearby. The stop had to be moved! Found dead in her little home, and mistakenly believed to be without relatives, she was buried at the expense of the local Roman Catholic parish, to whose annoyance it was later revealed that she had been a Baptist. Another eccentric figure familiar on the Road was a tramp known as Fortycoats because of his reluctance to 'cast a clout' when given a new, to him, garment.

The higher ground at Ormeau, past working-class Ballynafeigh, had its charms just like Malone. Early 19th century Rosetta House, was reputedly named after the daughter of its builder, William Napier, a whiskey distiller. Later it was the home of James Kennedy, muslin manufacturer. Its name was adopted for the neighbourhood.

Estate agent R. J. Mcconnell was selling houses to well-to-do professionals at Rosetta from the 1880s. (£700 bought a house there in 1890.) The extension of the tramline to Hampton Park in 1885 encouraged building in upper Ormeau.

The red-brick residence behind the cottages, a 'cottage villa' with deep roofs and impressively tall chimneys, was built about 1875 for John Coyle, a grocer on the lower Ormeau Road (Thomas Jackson and Son architects) and is one of two (the other backs on to it from Carolan Road). The accommodation is presently divided into four flats.

Rosetta

Until the 20th century Newtownbreda was a village with cottages, school and church. Its churchyard might have provoked thoughts in visitors akin to Gray's in his famous 'Elegy'. The tram, the car and urban expansion brought the village under the wing of Belfast.

Knockbreda, the parish, owes its name to the union of Knock and Breda brought about in the reign of Charles II. The church at Breda, in today's Belvoir Park, was in ruins by 1622 and worshippers had to travel to Knock.

In 1733 Arthur Hill, the squire at Breda, offered a two acre site for a church and his mother, Viscountess Midleton, met the cost of building it. Lady Ikkerin, at Castle Hill, opposed this transfer of the focus of the parish. However at a meeting of parishioners she was heavily outvoted and the bishop, having viewed both locations, decided in favour of Newtownbreda. The lady's appeal to Primate Boulter also failed.

The design of the church is credited to the German born Richard Cassels, or Castle, responsible for Leinster House in Dublin. The church was consecrated on 7th August, 1737.

Externally the building is in a simple Georgian Classical style, with a Gibbsian surround to the west door. The chancel was enlarged by the addition of a rounded sanctuary in 1883.

Electric lighting was installed in 1924 courtesy of the Purdy family, parishioners, who had their own private source, mains electricity not yet having got as far as Newtownbreda. Some of the oil lamps which had hitherto lit the building went to shed light in the church on Rathlin Island.

The squires – the Hills and later the Batesons (Lord Deramore) – had their pew in the north transept, enjoying the comfort of their own fireplace. The rectory pew opposite must have been well filled in the days of the Rev. John Kinahan (rector 1824-66): he fathered eight sons and eight daughters.

Oddly enough it was only recently thought necessary to install a lightning conductor on the spire. Perhaps the Vestry had lost confidence in the Almighty's ability to continue looking after the oldest church building still in use in South Belfast.

Knockbreda Church

South Belfast - a History of its People

PLANTERS: CHICHESTERS AND HILLS

The O'Neills of Clannaboye, who had reigned for centuries in the region which included the land on which South Belfast would be built, and who had fought the English government for possession of the castle of Belfast, lost their territories by confiscation and sale in the early 1600s. Planters from across the water took possession.

Oxford educated Sir Arthur Chichester had led an active life before he came to Ireland in 1599: he served on one of Drake's expeditions to the West Indies and under Henry IV of France, who knighted him. James I's grant of Belfast does not seem to have

filled him with enthusiasm because he was soon talking of disposing of it for a very small sum of money. His duties as Lord Deputy of Ireland (from 1604) often kept him away from the town but he initiated the rebuilding of the castle. He also provided himself with a   . country place on the Lagan which came to be known as Ormeau from the French word for the young elm trees he planted there. The 1611 Plantation Commissioners' Report noted that Sir Arthur *"hath* (there) *impaled a Parke of three myle compasse where he intendeth to buyld a house of lyme and stone"*. As an incomer he needed to have an eye to defence and his house at Ormeau was given *"a rampier of earth and soddes and a deep ditch standing full of water"*.

He was able to travel to Ormeau by water via a canal from his boathouse at the castle, the *'New Cutt River'* and the Lagan. Sir Arthur was created Baron Chichester of Belfast in 1612 and died in 1625. His only son having died in infancy, the estates passed to his brother Edward from whom the Earls and Marquesses of Donegall descend.

Since the Chichesters were largely absentees throughout the 18th century the cottage at Ormeau was let, but George Augustus, second Marquess, found it necessary to remove himself and his family to Belfast to escape his creditors in England, establishing himself in Donegall Place and at Ormeau, where the house was extended in the 1820s. He employed William Vitruvius Morrison as architect. He died at Ormeau in 1844 leaving his heir to pay off debts of £400,000, millions in modern terms. His ability to avoid paying his creditors earned him the nickname of 'Lord Done-em-all'.

Lord Donegall's sporting interests included horse-racing and yachting. He had a racecourse on land now covered by Haypark Avenue and neighbouring streets. Both sports lend themselves to betting and gambling debts added to his Lordship's financial difficulties.

After his death the family gave up Ormeau. A sale of contents was held in 1857. Damaged by a fire in 1861, it was demolished a few years later: John Robb bought the bricks to extend his clothing emporium in Castle Place. The Chichesters built a new residence, Belfast Castle, on the slopes of Cave Hill. After a scheme to build at Ormeau what would have been Belfast's first garden suburb was abandoned, the Belfast Corporation acquired 175 acres there from the Donegall estate and

allocated 100 of them to be the town's first public park, which opened at Easter 1871. Some of the remaining land was used for housing: Park Road and North and South Parades.

The 2nd Marquess had married Anna, the illegitimate daughter of an Irish baronet, Sir Edward May, who used the relationship to the advantage of both himself and his family. May Street, May's Field are reminders of the connection.

The charter granted to Belfast by James I in 1613 established a town government of a sovereign (mayor) and twelve burgesses, of whom Sir Moyses Hill, a planter from Devon, was probably the leading figure. Sir Moyses leased land at Malone and Stranmillis from Arthur Chichester and built *"a stronge fort"* on both, at strategic points on the Lagan. The lease seems to have been a sound investment. In 1634 a traveller admired a *"brave plantation which it is said doth yield him* (Moses' son, Arthur) *a £1,000 per annum"*. Hill's tenants were paying five or six shillings an acre in rent *"for good*

ploughing land, which is now clothed with excellent corn."

Moyses Hill died at Hillhall, built on land bought from Con O'Neill, in 1630. He had also acquired Ballynafeigh indirectly from O'Neill. Arthur Hill sold Ballynafeigh to Edward, Viscount Chichester in the 1630s.

The Hills extended their territory in other areas of County Down and managed to hold on to their estates at the restoration of the monarchy in spite of the fact that Arthur Hill had served under Cromwell's government. From that time they concentrated their interests at Hillsborough. A branch of the family developed an estate at Belvoir on the eastern side of the Lagan in the 18th century, taking the title of Viscount Dungannon. The old village of Breda, standing within the walls of the new park, was demolished and Newtownbreda took its place. Arthur Hill-Trevor, Viscount Dungannon, died in 1771 and was buried in a mausoleum in the old graveyard in his park where he lay undisturbed until vandals broke into it in 1951. His daughter Anna married the 1st Earl of Mornington and produced distinguished sons in Arthur, Duke of Wellington, and Richard, Marquess Wellesley. Annadale is called after her and the connection has been extended through the name of a new avenue, Mornington, and an apartment block on the upper Ormeau Road, Anna Hill. The eighteenth century Annadale Hall was destroyed by fire in 1921, having survived an earlier attack by suffragettes.

The Hill-Trevors were succeeded at Belvoir Park by the Batesons, later Lords Deramore. They went to live on their English estates at the end of the 19th century, apparently because the Lord Deramore of the day objected to the establishment of a mental hospital at Purdysburn, and the house was let to W. H. Wilson, one of the 'big four' of Harland and Wolff.

A less important figure among the planters was Henry le Squire who was given a lease of land at Stranmillis in about 1639 – the Hills appear to have given up their lease there early. His grant of land gave him licence to erect two corn mills *on the strand'*. This has been used to explain Stranmillis as a reference to le Squire's mills, though Gaelic scholars reject this interpretation. One of the hills surrounding Belfast, Squire's, is named after Henry.

BLUE AND WHITE PLAQUES

A walk along a street is always enlivened by finding a plaque distinguishing the residence of one who made a name in art, literature, science, or whatever. South Belfast, courtesy of the Ulster History Circle, offers the pleasure of such discoveries. In most cases the actual building is still in situ; where the original has been replaced the plaque – now somewhat distanced from its subject – has been attached to the new structure.

William Thomson, Baron Kelvin of Largs, was born in College Square East in 1824 where a plaque marks the site of the vanished Georgian terrace house. His father taught at 'Inst.' before being appointed to a chair in Mathematics at Glasgow University, where William began his education at the age of eleven. In 1846, aged 22, he was appointed Professor of Natural Philosophy at Glasgow, a position he held for 53 years. He was the first to define the Absolute Thermodynamic Scale of Temperature, the units of which are degrees Kelvin. His researches into the transmission of electric currents led to the successful laying of an Atlantic cable in 1866, for which he was knighted. His cable patents, along with many inventions, made him a fortune. Widely honoured, he died in 1907 and was buried in Westminster Abbey. His native city has commemorated his achievements with a statue in the Botanic Gardens. The inscription reads: *"Pre-eminent in Elucidating The Laws of Nature and in applying Them to the Service of Man."*

Close to the site of the Kelvin plaque is one to a man of very different tastes, Robert Shipboy McAdam (1808-1895). A brilliant linguist, he became a leading figure in the Irish Language Movement, having learnt Irish at 'Inst.'

Co-founder of the Ulster Gaelic Society and founder-editor of the Ulster Journal of Archaeology, he organised the collection of material for an English-Irish dictionary. With his brother he established the Soho Iron Foundry.

Robert Lynd, son of the minister of May Street Presbyterian Church, was educated at 'Inst.' and Queen's College, Belfast. A journalist, he was literary editor of the 'Daily News' from 1913-1947. He was a regular contributor to the 'New Statesman' and 'John o' London's Weekly'. His 'Dr Johnson and Company' won wide acclaim. He was awarded the 'Sunday Times Gold Medal' for belles lettres in 1932. A typical 'Lyndism' was:– *If we did not make mistakes there would be nothing in the world to laugh at. Hence, if we regard laughter as a blessing, we should pay a tribute to error.*"

Under the influence of F .J. Bigger he became a nationalist, supporting Sinn Fein in his writings and teaching Irish classes in London. A plaque marks his former home in Windsor Avenue.

For many Belfast folk William Conor is the painter par excellence of 'ordinary' people. After studying at the Government School of Design he took up an apprenticeship as a poster designer with the Belfast firm of David Allen. He was employed as a government artist during both World Wars. He explained that he liked to carry a newspaper as cover and behind it he would *"garner many happy impressions"* on his sketchpad unknown to his subjects. 'The Studio' noted that in Conor *"Belfast has a painter of genius"* and suggested that he could not have painted anywhere else. The studio he occupied from 1944 to 1959 on the Stranmillis Road is adorned with a plaque.

James Young was Ulster's star comic during the '60s and early '70s. Discovered by Sir Tyrone Guthrie, Young won acclaim for the characters he created, many of them based on people he met as a rent collector on the Shankill, Crumlin and Falls Roads, Mrs O'Condriac, the Cherry Valley Woman and Orange Lily. 'A clown with a conscience', he would end his television shows during the 'Troubles' with an urgent appeal to his viewers to *"Stap fightin'"*.

A plaque marks his childhood home in Fernwood Street, Ormeau Road.

A plaque on the old Victoria College building, Lower Crescent, bears the name of Margaret Byers. Born 1832, she married the Rev. John Byers, a missionary, and sailed with him to Shanghai. On the day before her son's birth her husband was pronounced terminally ill. As soon as possible after her baby was born she decided the three of them must return home. Unfortunately her husband died eight days after the ship reached New York. Margaret was a widow and a mother before she was twenty. Determined to make her own way in the world she established a school for young ladies first of all in Cookstown, then in Belfast. The Lower Crescent premises were opened in 1874 and the school renamed Victoria College in 1887 in honour of Queen Victoria's Golden Jubilee (with the Queen's permission). Most important for the further education of women Mrs Byers established a collegiate department to prepare students for the Arts examinations of the Royal University of Ireland. Her aim, she declared, was *"to provide for girls an education adapted to their wants as thorough as that afforded to boys in schools of the highest order."*

The citation accompanying the honorary doctorate awarded by Trinity College, Dublin, described her as:– *"the pride and glory of the great city of the North, who not only there but throughout our whole island in word and deed, with energy and wisdom, has stood in the forefront of a great and praiseworthy revolution."*

Another exceptional woman on South Belfast's register of the famous is Mary Ann McCracken whose story is told elsewhere in this book.

The most recently honoured South Belfast resident is Thomas Andrews of Messrs Harland and Wolff, chief designer of the 'Titanic'. He and his wife, Helen, née Barbour, of Dunmurry, set up home in Windsor Avenue in 1908, where the plaque has been installed. He sailed with the great liner on her maiden voyage. When he realised that she had been fatally holed by the iceberg he helped to organise the evacuation of passengers. Epitomising Chaucer's hero, the *"verray, parfit gentil knyght"*, he went down with his ship.

A member of an aristocratic family Vere Henry Foster, 1819-1909, abandoned a diplomatic service career to bring relief to victims of the Great Famine. The rest of his life and most of his wealth were devoted to good works. Having toured widely to see for himself the effects of famine he came to the conclusion that assisted emigration was the answer to the problems of over-population and poverty in Ireland. Learning of the harsh treatment of passengers on emigrant ships he sailed steerage to find out for himself. His protests led to his being knocked down by an irate ship's officer and hospitalisation in New York. He spent thousands of pounds of his own money in assisting young men and women to begin new lives in America and Canada where he originated groups to receive them.

Education was the great interest of his later life. The Vere Foster copybooks, by which children learnt to write elegantly while absorbing moral teaching through the axioms they copied, are his chief memorial. Printed by the Belfast firm of Marcus Ward, they were given free to poor children and were to cost no more than a penny to the others.

He died in lodgings at 115 Great Victoria Street where a plaque once commemorated this 'Prince of Philanthropists' He is buried in the City Cemetery where his grave has been restored by the Irish National Teachers' Organisation which he helped to form.

Born in Ayrshire, Scotland, in 1840 John Boyd Dunlop set up as a vet in Belfast in his late twenties. He did not invent the pneumatic tyre but rather perfected it. He developed the first practical form in 1888 to enable his invalid son to cycle in comfort over

Belfast's cobbles, according to one story, or to ease the transport of sick animals, according to another. His invention reduced the effort required to move a vehicle and encouraged the development of cycling as a pastime. Tyres were made in Belfast, then in Dublin. Dunlop died in 1921. A commemorative plate once adorned his premises, long since demolished, in May Street.

A plaque on a house in Fitzwilliam Place, University Road, distinguishes the birthplace of James Owen Hannay, clergyman, Protestant nationalist, Gaelic Leaguer and, as George A. Birmingham, prolific novelist: he produced more than 50 comic novels in which he gently satirised the Ireland of the early 20th century. Like Synge and O'Casey he found that nationalists were not always amused by his depiction of the Irish and he was turfed out of the Gaelic League. A stage version of his 'General John Regan' presented in Westport, where he was rector, resulted in his being burnt in effigy.

And what names might be added to the register? Certainly John Hewitt, poet and writer on art, who lived in Mount Charles and on Stockman's Lane, and Paul Henry, painter, whose childhood home was on University Road, deserve the honour.

RESTING PLACES

The blue and white plaque trail may be extended by visits to the cemeteries of South Belfast. The oldest, Knockbreda, contains the graves of some of the less well known figures behind the political events of the rebellious 1790s. Members of the Society of United Irishmen buried here include Henry Haslett, a founder member of the Belfast branch, the Rev. Robert Acheson and William Simms, secretary of the branch. Simms was one of the group that met Wolfe Tone at McArt's Fort in 1795 when they swore *"never to desist until Ireland was free."* Samuel Neilson, also of that group, and the most important of the Belfast members, was arrested on the eve of the Rebellion. He was released from prison in Scotland on condition that he go

into exile. He died in the United States. His wife and some of his children are interred at Knockbreda.

Those who supported the government at this time of trouble are represented at Knockbreda by John Brown, several times sovereign (mayor) of Belfast, and Cortland Macgregor Skinner, both yeomanry officers. Skinner restored order in Ballynahinch after the battle there.

Included among the number of Belfast's industrial and commercial families who found last resting places in Knockbreda cemetery are Atkinson (drink), Riddel (hardware), Grimshaw (cotton, banking), Kennedy (linen), Bateson (banking), Blakiston-Houston (banking), MacAdam (ironworks), and Cunningham and Greg (leading figures in 18th century Belfast commerce). Belfast's most important mid-Victorian architect, Sir Charles Lanyon, designer of Queen's College and the Custom House, is also to be found among the illustrious dead at Knockbreda.

The little cemetery at Balmoral was

opened in 1855 by a private company. A prospectus published by the proprietors reminds us of Victorian ideas of seemliness when it came to the burial of the dead: *"Although ground is set apart at low rate for persons who have not the means of purchasing in fee, yet the main design is to put it within the power of the man of taste, of even humble circumstances, to obtain for his remains and those of his heirs, a retired, secure and elegant resting place."*

There is a distinctly Presbyterian complexion to the place. By 1900 the remains of 24 Presbyterian ministers had been buried here, the most famous being the Rev. Dr Henry Cooke whose funeral in 1868 was described as *"in all respects like a royal or imperial demonstration"*, 154 carriages following the cortege. Mourners included the Presbyterian Moderator, the Church of Ireland Primate and the Roman Catholic Bishop of Down and Connor. The grave of the Rev. John Edgar, social reformer and temperance campaigner, is also to be found here. There is a strong Indian connection too, missionaries and civil servants, among them James Glasgow, principal translator of the Bible into Gujarati. William Batt, Jr, architect of many houses in Malone, also lies in Balmoral cemetery.

The prospectus's promise that *"As the ground of the Cemetery will be chiefly in the hands of proprietors, it can never become a nursery for vermin, nor present the characteristics of old, overcrowded graveyards"* was one that the proprietors could not keep. The cemetery is now in the care of Belfast Corporation.

In nearby Balmoral Avenue there is the Society of Friends (Quakers) burial ground. The Society opened a meeting house in Frederick Street in the town early in the 19th century; since there was no ground adjacent for a graveyard, and the Friends had their own distinctive practices relating to the burial of the dead which ruled out the use of a public cemetery, a site was found on the Lisburn Road in what was then open country. At first there were no gravestones but after about 1850 plain stones of uniform size and shape were allowed, the inscription being confined to name, age and date of death. Eulogies were forbidden, Quakers believing all were equal in the sight of God.

However not everyone is equal in the eyes of their neighbours and two names are worthy of note at Balmoral: Forster Green, tea and coffee merchant, philanthropist and founder of the Forster Green Hospital for Consumption and Chest Diseases at Fortbreda; Thomas Jackson, architect, whose buildings included the Old Museum in College Square North, St. Malachy's Roman Catholic Church, Alfred Street, Victoria Hall, May Street, and Queen's Elms. His son, and partner, Anthony Thomas, was also interred at Balmoral.

Adjoining the Friends' cemetery is a Presbyterian church which although on the Lisburn Road is known as Malone because that name seemed more appropriate when the congregation was established in 1835 in what was then a rural area. It too had its cemetery, long since closed. Among those buried there was an African servant of the Wilsons of Maryville, Malone. One wonders how she came to Belfast and did her race make her unique in the town.

THE POOR

The rich and famous feature largely in his book. What about those who were not so successful, the poor and obscure who lived in Cromac, Sandy Row and streets off the Lisburn and Donegall Roads? Photographs taken by R. J. Welch in Cromac in 1912 show living conditions for some of them to have been at their most basic.

For many at that time the working week was long – 68 hours for a carter, 60 for a tram conductor. Wages for those without a trade skill were low enough to earn end-of-the-19th century Belfast the title of 'cheap labour capital of the United Kingdom'. Periodic depression put workers on short time or made them unemployed. In times of hardship people shared accommodation. Recourse was had to pawnshops (six in Sandy Row in 1890), charities and money-lenders, even prostitution. People queued at bakeries like McWatters' in Cromac Street to buy stale bread at greatly reduced prices. Coke could be had at the Gasworks as a cheap substitute for coal. Wives often had no alternative but to work to supplement their husband's wages. The children might contribute to the family budget by running errands, selling flowers, sticks or newspapers. The last could bring in six or seven shillings a week. For those at the bottom of the social pyramid, the permanently unemployed though able-bodied, the aged, the feeble or those with no one to look after them, there was the Workhouse, a place of dread to all.

During the Famine applications for admission to the Workhouse hugely increased as people fled starvation in the countryside. Nassau Senior, Assistant Poor Law Commissioner, described the Belfast establishment as the most overcrowded he had seen, although it was well managed. In fact a building designed for 1,000 was squeezing in 2,825 people in April 1848. Overcrowding forced the Guardians, much against their will, to pay outdoor relief. The middle class Guardians had a vested interest as ratepayers in keeping the poor rate down; they believed that the poor would only abuse relief if it were offered too freely.

The Board of Guardians provided a ready focus for the discontent of the unemployed, especially in times of economic depression. In 1926 a protest against the parsimony of the Guardians in the payment of outdoor relief took place outside the Workhouse. In defence of its policy the Clerk of the Union wrote smugly that the Board *"has steadfastly resisted pressure from various sources to distribute outdoor relief to all able-bodied applicants and thereby has prevented many abuses"*.

A much bigger event was the Outdoor Relief Strike which lasted a fortnight in October 1932 and led to rioting in the west and east of the city. Workers employed on distress relief schemes demanded a full week's work, an end to payment in kind and higher wages. Seven thousand men accompanied a deputation to the

Workhouse. The gates were locked against them and a strong force of police took up position outside. Baulked, the crowd chanted slogans mocking the Guardians and blocked the road by lying down on the tramlines. One Guardian suffered the indignity of having to climb over a wall to get inside. Those taking part in a demonstration next day defied a police ban and were driven back into Sandy Row, where shops were looted. These protests brought Protestant and Catholic workers together in a short-lived show of unity. Ironically, Belfast churches were holding harvest thanksgiving services at this time when thousands were going hungry.

In 1948 the Poor Law system was shut down and the Workhouse buildings were transferred to the new Hospitals Authority to be known thereafter as the City Hospital.

But before that happened a new concept in provision for the poor, the unemployed, the sick and the aged, the Welfare State, was developing, beginning with David Lloyd George's introduction of old age pensions, health and unemployment insurance in 1909.

EDUCATION

Education is the best ticket to a better quality of life. The census returns of 1901 show South Belfast to have had the lowest rate of illiteracy of the four quarters of the city. When one considers the educational provision in the area and the class structure one can understand why this was so.

The most important educational establishment in South Belfast is the University opened in 1849 as Queen's College. The streets around it attracted middle class professionals, academics, doctors, clergy and businessmen. The ambience was right for setting up schools for the education of the offspring of such folk. The wealthier sent their sons to English public schools. For those educated at home there were co-educational Methodist College and Victoria College for girls. Both schools have sent out men and women who proved their worth in the city and beyond. Former alumni of Victoria, for example, include Helen Waddell, formidable scholar, author of *The Desert Fathers*; Bee Duffell, actress; Beatrice Grimshaw, explorer and traveller in the South Pacific; Thelma Hopkins, Olympic and Empire Games medallist. Victoria is the longest established girls school in the British Isles. It united with Richmond Lodge in 1987.

Richmond, a private establishment run by the Hardy sisters, was at first a school for boys, though taking a few girls. Its earliest pupils included Forrest Reid (novelist), Robert Lynd (journalist) and Herbert Dixon (first Lord Glentoran, politician). When the school moved to Rupert Lodge, Malone Road, it became Richmond Lodge High School for Girls. Richmond girls were encouraged to look beyond their priviliged world to those not so well off. The first nursery school in Ireland, Arellian, was set up by former pupils of Richmond in the Sandy Row area in 1928. Later, under headmistress Miss Maxwell, they turned their eyes yet further afield through the Council for Education in World Citizenship.

Two other South Belfast schools now operate as one, Princess Gardens and Ashleigh House, united at Dunmurry as Hunterhouse College. The name commemorates the founder of the former, Miss Hunter. 'Inst.' opened a preparatory department, Inchmarlo, in Marlborough Park in 1917. When numbers made larger premises necessary the school moved to Mount Randal, Cranmore Park, in 1935.

At one time private schools, no doubt of varying quality, abounded. One such was the Educational Establishment for the Daughters of Gentlemen in College Square North run by the Misses Black. It offered the inducement of half price travel to school on the trams. The Shaftesbury House Tutorial College (known as Renshaw's after the proprietor) was in operation until the 1980s; Garvey College, Botanic Avenue, was a similar establishment. Schools such as the last two were often dismissed as 'crammers', a charge they would have denied, but their survival

did depend on their pupils' successes in public examinations.

Under the old system the majority of the children of South Belfast got their education in the National, mainly church, schools. The hope that such schools, established from 1831, would be non-denominational was not realised because the churches preferred to control the schools where their young people were taught. Buildings often doubled as church halls. The general pattern was the large schoolroom where all classes met, pupils moving from station to station as the day's programme dictated. The education on offer was not always completely free and the children might have to contribute to the cost of heating the building. The latter was a source of resentment in poor families with more than one child at a school, as one who had been through the system has testified. Those who did not pay up promptly were publicly shamed.

The modern set-up began in 1923 with legislation enabling churches to transfer their schools to new authorities

with responsibility for educational provision. As a result many sub-standard buildings were closed and new ones built. The star performer in this operation was Reginald Wilshere, architect to the Belfast Education Authority, who designed the first modern schools in Ireland, with separate classrooms and specialist subject rooms. Botanic is an example in South Belfast.

The Roman Catholic Church refused to transfer its schools, insisting that *"the only satisfactory system of education for Catholics is one wherein Catholic children are taught in Catholic schools by Catholic teachers under Catholic auspices"*. Thus division on religious lines was perpetuated.

Private funding enabled the Christian Brothers to open a boys school on Oxford Street in 1874 and Belfast hotelier Matthew Bowen met the cost of a *"Young* (Catholic) *Ladies School"* in Sussex Place. A primary school was opened in connection with St. Brigid's Church on Derryvolgie Avenue. New secondary schools, Aquinas College and

St. Joseph's, are located on the Ravenhill Road.

A bold attempt to bridge the sectarian divide (integration could not be enforced) took place in 1980 with the establishment of Lagan College as an integrated school. It now enjoys attractive new premises at Lisnabreeny on the fringe of South Belfast and has been joined in the field of integrated education by a number of primary and secondary schools including Cranmore Primary and Malone College.

The years following World War II saw secondary education prospects for poorer families improve. The number of scholarships to grammar schools increased; a new grammar school, Grosvenor High, was opened in January 1945. But it was not until 1947 that 'Educational Reconstruction in Northern Ireland' was achieved by which primary education was to be completed at age 11, after which pupils would proceed to secondary (including grammar and technical) level. Annadale and Carolan joined the grammar schools already in existence in South Belfast. These two have been united as Wellington College.

The Deaf and Dumb and Blind Institution, once a feature of the lower Lisburn Road, and opened in 1845, was the culmination of a number of projects to provide education and industrial training for such people. Lanyon's Tudor-style building was demolished in 1963 and the school relocated at Jordanstown. Other work among the deaf was done by the Ulster Institute in Fisherwick Place of which the first superintendent was the Rev. Francis Maginn. The son of a County Cork clergyman, he lost his hearing at the age of five when he fell victim to scarlet fever. As a missionary to the deaf Maginn travelled widely, helping deaf people to find employment and making sure the sleepy heads among them got to work of a morning. The Rev. John Kinghan, Presbyterian minister and principal of the Institution, established a Mission to the Deaf in 1857. The work continues today in the Kinghan Church, Botanic Avenue.

South Belfast was the location for three 'special' schools, variously known as reformatories, borstals or industrial schools. Hampton House, Balmoral Avenue, opened sometime before 1880 with accommodation for 100 girls considered to be in need of care, but who had not been convicted of any crime. They were known locally as 'Hampers'. Malone Training School, established 1860 as Malone Protestant Reformatory (religious segregation operated in this field too) on land between the Ulster Railway and the Bog Meadows, took in boys. The borstal section is now located at Woburn, Millisle. Junior boys, at first accommodated on a training ship, 'Grampian', in Belfast Lough, returned to land in 1883, at Fox Lodge, Ravenhill Road, and later at the Model Farm Buildings which were renamed the Balmoral Industrial School. The School is presently at Rathgael, Bangor.

EMPLOYMENT

Though there has been industry in South Belfast the area has always been essentially residential.

The earliest industrial enterprise was at New Forge in the 17th century where a plentiful supply of wood for charcoal encouraged iron-smelting. Later three industries had a strong connection with the district: linen-finishing, brick-making and the manufacture of mineral waters.

The Bedford Street/Ormeau Avenue area was once lined with premises where the linen industry prepared its goods for sale. The workers there thought themselves superior to those who toiled in spinning mills and weaving factories. Certainly their working conditions were pleasanter. One hundred thousand miles of cloth were sold each year in the 1880s in Ulster when linen was king. Artificial fibres dethroned the monarch in the 20th century and warehouses such as Bryson House are being put to other uses now. The premises of Messrs Ewart, once a giant of the industry, are closed up, awaiting a future. Nostalgically, perhaps, the panels covering the windows illustrate the various stages in the production of linen.

In the words of an old street song:

This jewel that houses our hopes
and our fears
Was knocked up from the swamp in the
last hundred years.

The 'swamp' provided material to be made into bricks and South Belfast provided many of them. Arthur Chichester rebuilt the castle of Belfast in the early 1600s, using bricks. He ordered twelve hundred thousand to be made, more than he would need: the rest went to build other houses and thus the use of bricks was firmly established. Belfast is a brick city.

In the 17th and 18th centuries bricks were made from the material of the slobland, sleech. In the early 1700s they were being manufactured in 'Brick Kiln Land' *"situate beyond the Brick Kiln Bridge on the right hand of the way leading to Malone"*, i.e. near the Boyne Bridge in Sandy Row. Brick yards are shown clustered around Brick Hall beside the Blackstaff on a map of 1791. Brick yards were also to be found in Cromac.

The material used in the 19th century, producing bricks reddish in colour, was boulder clay to be found on both sides of the Lagan near Stranmillis where the Haypark, Marquis, Prospect, Annadale and Laganvale Works were located. Because the deposits were shallow they were soon worked out. Gypsum in the clay accounts for the white powdery deposit often seen on bricks.

The old-fashioned way was to burn bricks in clamps, the kiln was a later development. One is shown near Ormeau Park on a map of 1864. (The homeless found a kiln from which the bricks had recently been removed a warm place in which to sleep.) In 1888 Messrs H. and J. Martin, owners of the largest brick-making business in Ireland and major players in the City's end-of-century building boom, were producing 60,000 bricks a day at their Haypark and Prospect Works. The Annadale Brick Company advertised *'Wire cut, Fancy and Ornamental Bricks, Ridge-Tiles, Terra Cotta and Field-drain Pipes'* in the 1890 Directory.

South Belfast's brick fields have all been built over. The building industry now looks to Dungannon and Coalisland for supplies.

Good supplies of excellent water lie deep under Belfast in beds of Triassic sandstone but, except for a few places like Fountainville and Cromac, the water was not much used for domestic purposes until the 19th century. Wells were sunk to tap these supplies (Ross's well in Victoria Square was 420 feet deep) and an industry developed in 'aerated waters', claimed as a Belfast invention. Twenty-five manfacturers are listed in 1890. Messrs Grattan, established in Cromac in 1825, were the pioneers. Their new premises on Great Victoria Street (1883) were equipped with machinery of the *"newest and best design"*; the apparatus was lined with silver (no lead tubing); the fittings were of silver. Wheeler, Corry, Cantrell and Cochrane, Ross became household names. Corry's advertised *"Gold Medal Aerated Beverages Prepared Exclusively from the Limpid Waters of Corry and Company's celebrated Cromac Spring. Guaranteed*

free from metallic or other impurity." Carbon dioxide gas was added to the water along with sweetener, flavouring and colouring to create a variety of soft drinks.

The products of the various companies, lemonade, ginger ale, seltzer waters, etc., were exported to cheer the lives, the adveriements lead us to believe, of administrators throughout the British Empire. Messrs Ross claimed that their mineral waters were *"Recommended by the Faculty, Medical Journals and most eminent Analytical Chemists of the Day."* Sparkling Montserrat was especially recommended for the gouty and rheumatic.

The Cromac waters proved to be equally good for whiskey distilling.

A manufacturing 'curiosity' operated for a time at Stranmillis where Frederick King and Co., produced 'Mrs Edwards' Dessicated Soup'. Believed to be the first powdered soup, it was used to thicken sauces, etc. And it was made according to 'a secret process'.

Vulcanite Ltd also operated at Stranmillis, producing bitumen roofing tiles, damp-proof courses and grey felt paper. Houses built in Laganvale Street for its workers were given flat roofs covered with the company's tiles.

HEALTH

Addressing the British Association for the Advancement of Science, meeting in Belfast in 1852, Dr Andrew Malcolm declared, *"Fever may be said to be endemic in this town".* He was referring to the old Belfast centred on the White Linen Hall. The movement of people to suburbs in South Belfast was inspired as much by a desire to find a healthy place in which to live as to have a fashionably new address.

'Healthy' and 'rural' were words used in publicising developments at Windsor in the 1850s. The governors of Methodist College emphasised the healthy location of the new school, though a few years earlier Dr Malcolm had noted of the nearby Friar's Bush cemetery that it was *"excessively overcrowded and were it not far removed from the town would certainly prove injurious to the public health of its immediate vicinity."*

'Fever' was the result of many factors: poor diet, overcrowding, inadequate water supply and sanitation, deficient housing, even illiteracy. The influx of people from the countryside to escape the Famine brought disease into Belfast. At that time the Union Infirmary was stretched beyond its limits and had to be enlarged. Sheds were erected in the Workhouse yards; the stables, strawhouse and a new piggery were called into service. Hospital accommodation elsewhere in town was quickly filled and temporary arrangements had to be made: a hospital was set up in the grounds of 'Inst.'

It would take decades to bring improvement and in the meantime the town fringes of South Belfast, Cromac and Sandy Row, remained very unhealthy. In August 1916 the City Medical Officer of Health noted that a very high percentage of the city's rubbish was not incinerated but dumped in pits at various sites, one of which was close to the back doors of houses in lower Sandhurst Gardens, Stranmillis. Foul water accumulated in the 20 feet deep pit and rats flourished. The street was found to have the highest death rate among children in the area.

Corporation regulations gradually established standards for new housing (especially provision of access for the removal of waste). Water from the Mournes brought many blessings. Public baths also contributed to safeguarding health in areas where houses did not have bathrooms; the Donegall Pass area benefited from such provision in Ormeau Avenue. But it would be the work of the Northern Ireland Housing Trust /Housing Executive in the late 20th century that would make all the difference to the living conditions of the working classes.

Consumption was the most consistent killer. Steps towards providing treatment climaxed in the setting up of the Hospital for Consumption and Diseases of the Chest at Fortbreda in 1896, largely through the generosity of tea merchant Forster Green after whom it was named.

In the opinion of some doctors fresh air was not given priority in the treatment of chest complaints. Professor Henry McCormac's belief in its efficacy landed him in the Police Court for breaking a patient's window with his umbrella to let in air.

Over the years the Lisburn Road became a focus for hospital building: the City, the Jubileee, the Abercorn, the Dufferin and Ava, the Samaritan and Musgrave Park, each with its own specialisation. Great Victoria Street and College Squares East and North once comprised Belfast's Harley Street, though some thought the Valley of the Shadow of Death a more appropriate name. The 1890 directory lists 29 medics with addresses there.

Famous among medical men were the Brownes, father and son, who between them gave 78 years of service to the Ophthalmic Hospital on Great Victoria

Street. The son, John Walton Browne, later knighted, was described by a patient as *"genial, with a dash of brutality and very little patience"*. One of the Purdons was responsible for setting up, on Donegall Pass, Belfast's first chest diseases dispensary. To Dr O'Neill Belfast owed higher standards in butcher's shops and in the quality of the meat supply.

But the one who gained greatest fame was William Whitla (1851-1933). A Queen's College graduate, he occupied the chair of Materia Medica there for 30 years. His *Elements of Pharmacy, Materia Medica and Therapeutics* was translated into 30 languages. In diagnosis he was said to be unequalled. Gifted with a sense of humour he awarded his students a holiday when they sang 'God save the King' on his appointment as an honorary physician to King George V. His daily reading was said to be the book of Psalms and the stock market reports. Keeping himself right with both worlds? Whitla's generosity is evident in his gifts: to his university (his home at Lennoxvale is now the Vice

Chancellor's Lodge; a large bequest built the Sir William Whitla Hall); to his city (the Whitla Medical Institute) and his school (Methodist College).

And let us not forget the baby, John William, so soon orphaned, born to Margaret Byers in Shanghai. He was destined to figure largely in Belfast's medical history as Professor of Midwifery at Queen's and specialist in diseases affecting women and children. Professor Byers' work earned him a knighthood.

The poor of Sandy Row and the Markets might not be able to afford to call in a doctor and recourse was had to traditional remedies. Coughs, sore throats, sprains, muscle pains, backache and warts were treated with various potions. Superstition sometimes played a part: the touch of a widow's wedding ring was said to cure ringworm. Treatment was not always painless: one method of 'drawing' a boil was said to reduce even strong men to tears. A person with the "gift" to cure a particular disease was highly valued. A visit to the Gasworks to breathe in the

sulphur fumes was recommended for victims of whooping cough.

SPORT

Sporting facilities abound in South Belfast: playing fields, parks, golf courses, tennis clubs, the river and a ski slope.

North of Ireland Football and Cricket Club, until recently located on the Ormeau Road, is the oldest club, the cricketing side being established in the winter of 1859. In its first season 'North' received an English club, played All-Ireland and All-England XIs and undertook an English tour.

The football section, rugby, was formed in the autumn of 1868. At that time rugby was largely unknown in Ireland except among men who had been educated at English public schools. Queen's College had a team, as did Trinity College, Dublin. North's first match began on 16th January, 1869 and was continued on two further Saturday afternoons until the winning team, Queen's College, had scored two goals. The number of players on a team had not yet been settled at 15: on the first afternoon 13 Northmen faced 18 Queen's men. The Club thrived: six North players were on the Irish international side against England in 1875. The first Irish international against Scotland was played at Ormeau in 1877.

The last major event at the Ormeau Road ground was on 12th August, 2001 when an Irish cricket XI met an Australian side. Unfortunately rain stopped play. The Club is now located at Orangefield.

Linfield Athletic Football Club was officially founded in March 1886 by workers of the Linfield Spinning Mill in Sandy Row and the Club's first pitch was 'The Meadow' behind the mill. The first match was against Distillery; Linfield won 6-5. At first membership was limited to Mill employees but this was given up in order to secure a wider pool of players. The Club might have been renamed Linfield Wanderers because it was 1904 before it found a permanent home by purchasing part of the Bog Meadows and building Windsor Park.

In the course of more than a century the 'Blues' have had their share of sporting heroes, players who justified the Club's choice of motto, *Audaces Fortuna Juvat* (Fortune favours the brave). Bob Milne, one of the earliest, won nine Irish Cup Medals and played 27 times for Ireland between 1894 and 1906. Joe 'Slip it to Joe' Bambrick, created a record by scoring six goals in one match (1930 against Wales). Tommy Dickson, known as 'The Duke of Windsor', led a team in 1961-2 which repeated the glorious achievement of 1921-2 by winning seven trophies.

Of the five golf courses in South Belfast Ormeau Park is the oldest, Mt Ober the youngest. Belvoir Park (1927) has hosted major tournaments but it was to Balmoral that glory came, in 1947, when the Club's professional, Fred Daly (later M.B.E.) won the British Open Championship at Hoylake, the only Irishman ever to do so. (His prize money? £150!) Daly began his golfing career as a caddy at Portrush, then served as club professional at Mahee and Lurgan before being lured to Balmoral at the princely wage of £5 a week, which made him the highest paid pro. in Ireland at the time. His achievements as a player, the Open, runner-up in the Open in 1948, equal third 1950 and '52, three times a member of the Ryder Cup team, etc., were recognised by his election to the Texaco Hall of Fame (1984).

At Upper Malone are the University's playing fields, the House of Sport (Sports Council for Northern Ireland) and the Belfast council-owned athletics track (developed to international standard) named after Northern Ireland's Golden Girl athlete, Mary Peters. Top athletes Linford Christie, Steve Ovett and Zola Budd have competed there.

Those with memories going back to the 1930s and early '40s will remember 'Ma' (Clara) Copley's boxing booth at the Chapel Fields, Alfred Street. Mrs Copley achieved the distinction of being the first woman to be licenced by the British Boxing Board of Control as a promoter. The fighters came from local clubs and from across the water. Some of them became famous, Jimmy Warnock, Spider Kelly and Rinty Monaghan, who held World, British, European and Commonwealth flyweight titles. Some were 'characters', like Cecil Creighton who was known as the birdman and swallowed live goldfish as part of his performance. He was not a very successful fighter, spending so much time down on the canvas that local wits declared that he had a cauliflower bum. Prizes were modest, five or ten shillings, but in the hungry '30s they were welcome. Asked to explain the later falling off in quality among local boxers Mick Ross, Ma's M.C., said, *"There are no hungry fighters today"*. Ma retired in 1942 when the Corporation raised the rent of the Ulster Hall which she was using after the Chapel Fields ceased to be available. The Belfast Telegraph noted that there was widespread regret at her *"enforced cessation"* after 11 years of *"fostering the sport"*.

One of Belfast's most successful tennis clubs, Y.M.C.A., established itself at Bladon in 1922, where it thrived for seventy years until the land was sold for housing in 1992. Competitions drew players from all over Ireland and several Club members served on the councils of the Ulster and Irish Lawn Tennis Associations.

An artificial slalom course for canoeing has been made on the river at Shaw's Bridge (Clement Wilson Park). Bowlers are catered for in public parks, Botanic and Ormeau, and on private greens, for example Shaftesbury Bowling Club on Annadale Avenue.

THE LAGAN

A river is a key factor in deciding the siting of a town. Paris has the Seine, London the Thames. A river, or rivers, determined the location of our town for it was where one, the Farset, flowed into another, the Lagan, that Belfast, (*Beal Feirsde* : the approach to, or the mouth of, the sandbank or ford) came into being. The town plan of 1685 clearly labels the Farset, not the Lagan,

'Belfast River'. And it was the Farset that dictated the layout of the early town, settling the curved shape and width of High Street. Ships docked where the Farset entered the Lagan. In the course of the 18th century the 'Belfast River' was covered over and so ceased to impinge on the minds of the townsfolk. The future lay with the Lagan, whose channel was straightened and deepened to accommodate the shipping that would establish Belfast as a great commercial centre. But that was down river from the old Long Bridge. What of the river upstream, Stranmillis wards?

A picture of Belfast from Lord Donegall's park at Ormeau portrays the Lagan winding towards the Long Bridge, the town on one side, Lagan village and Ballymacarrett, on the other. Parkland reaches down to the river. It is an idyllic, pre-Industrial Revolution scene. One could imagine the Lagan offering many sporting opportunities – fishing, swimming, boating – although that stretch was already in use as part of the Lagan Navigation. 'The Northern Whig' newspaper reported a *'fête champêtre'* at the Botanic Gardens in August, 1840 when the river was crowded with boats, some carrying musicians.

The 19th century development of Belfast put an end to such possibilities. Industrial pollution and the dumping of waste poisoned the waters. For example, the Blackstaff flowed into the Lagan at the Gasworks. In 1852 Dr Andrew Malcolm described the Blackstaff as *"the receptacle of the refuse of upwards of 400 houses, besides factories and public institutions where many hundreds congregate and reside"*. In the 1880s the young Paul Henry, visiting Ormeau Park, contrasted the *"wood full of magnificent trees, where we gathered bunches of wild hyacinths"*, with the river – *"how evil smelling were its waters although boys were bathing from the banks."*

A writer in the Belfast Book of 1929 described the river from the Ormeau Bridge: at low tide on the left was a broad mud flat, *"black and odoriferous"*, *"apparently the dumping ground for worn out hardware"*; the right side was

no better, *"here the bank is rough and broken … between the two there is a narrow and tortuous channel of muddy water."*

And what an amenity the Lagan could have been. A serious start to improving this stretch of the river was begun in the 1920s. The Corporation was empowered, as an unemployment relief scheme, to construct about three miles of 60 feet wide roadway along the river banks; a weir situated between the Albert and Ormeau Bridges was meant to keep the mudbanks permanently covered. A lock would enable river vessels to travel upstream and down. There were hopes of a boating reach. The banks were sloped and grassed, bushes and trees were planted. The Stranmillis Embankment, from Ormeau Bridge to the King's Bridge was completed in autumn 1929. It was subsequently continued to Lockview Road.

Though these improvements were an advance, seventy years on the river problem had to be tackled again. Part-financed by the European

Development Fund a huge clean-up operation was launched in the early 1990s. Since barges could not be used to carry away the material dredged up temporary causeways of stones were laid on the river bed to enable excavators to dig out the mud which was then loaded on lorries to be taken to cap the landfill site on the north foreshore of Belfast Lough. As the work progressed the causeways were resited for further digging. At the same time the banks were secured and water treatment equipment was installed.

The river between Stranmillis weir and the inner harbour of Belfast is now managed by the Laganside Corporation whose declared aim is to promote *"the recreational use of the River Lagan, particularly angling"*. Nine fishing stands have been set up at Annadale Embankment where anglers may try their luck at coarse fishing: roach, bream, mullet, sea and brown trout and even salmon apparently being on offer. Across the river from the stands are sheds where rowing clubs keep their boats. The Belfast Rowing Club opened a new clubhouse here, on Hay

Island, in 1977 after its position in Balfour Avenue, Lower Ormeau, had become untenable. Nearby is a popular pub-restaurant, Cutters Wharf.

Belfast now has a river that is cleaner and safer, and attractive to look at. A new walkway on the town side links Ormeau and Albert Bridges and gives access to the Gasworks business park. Pleasure boats ply; an attempt has been made to persuade workers to commute by river to and from Stranmillis; new apartment blocks at Stranmillis and on the Ormeau Embankment make the river a selling point. A flight of steps down to the river in front of the latter leaves one wondering if the planners had gondolas in mind. A water sports centre operates at Albert Bridge.

AIR SERVICE

In October 1923 the Belfast Corporation declared itself in favour of establishing an airlink between Belfast and a suitable city in England. Lord Mayor Sir William Turner was particularly keen. £15,000 was voted for initial expenditure. The first site to be explored, an old polo ground at Castlereagh, was rejected as too expensive. Land, 50 acres, was found at Malone adjacent to Balmoral golf course.

The flight operators, Northern Airlines, hoped to accelerate the delivery of English newspapers to the Province, to develop an airmail service (a halfpenny would be added to the cost of the stamp) and to carry passengers when space was available (single fare £3). The inaugural flight took place on 30 April, 1924 with the Lord Mayor and High Sheriff of Belfast as passengers. Manchester had been proposed as the destination but because of difficulties there Liverpool, within two hours' flying time from Belfast, was chosen instead, the planes landing on Aintree race-course. The first regular flight was on May 2nd. The route took the planes, DH 50s, across the Down coast between Groomsport and Bangor to the Mull of Kintyre, over Luce Bay and the Solway Firth and down the Cumberland coast to Southport before turning inland to Liverpool and Aintree.

However it was soon clear that all was not well. Corporation minutes noted that there was no hangar for the planes and the airfield was liable to flooding. Lack of adequate weather reports caused problems. Flying attracted few passengers and the business community showed little interest in the mail service. The UK's first municipal aerodrome closed down after about a year and the airfield was let for grazing.

WARTIME

Memorial plaques and stained glass windows in churches remember the men and women who answered the call to arms in the years 1914 to 1918: of the 106 who volunteered from St. Bartholomew's parish, Stranmillis, 24 made the supreme sacrifice. Many who had enlisted in the Ulster Volunteer Force, for whom Malone Road South African War veteran Fred Crawford had run guns into Larne in April 1914, found themselves fighting Germans instead of Home Rule. The Volunteers played an important role in Kitchener's army as the 36th (Ulster) Division. Men who had received their military training in Queen's University Officer Training Corps were commissioned in the course of the war. The University's war memorial lists 254 of them, including 54 doctors and medical students.

One Queen's man achieved the accolade of the Victoria Cross. He was John Alexander Sinton who served as a doctor with the Indian Expeditionary Force in Mesopotamia. The citation reads *"although shot through both arms and through the side, he refused to go to hospital, and remained, as long as daylight lasted, attending to his duties under very heavy fire. In three previous actions Captain Sinton displayed the utmost courage"*. Sinton survived the war and practised as a G.P. for many years on the Stranmillis Road. Captain the Rev. James G. Paton, later minister of Malone Presbyterian Church and Moderator of the General Assembly, served as chaplain with the 10th Royal Inniskilling Fusiliers from 1915-1919, being decorated three times (Military Cross and two bars).

Wooden huts were erected at the University to serve as an Ulster Volunteer Force hospital. They were taken over by various University departments when the hospital was moved to Craigavon House after the war. The Star and Garter Association built houses for ex-servicemen on the Saintfield Road and Galwally House became a U.V.F. hospital whose blue-uniformed patients were familiar figures in upper Ormeau.

The war against Hitler and the Axis powers was most deeply felt in 1941 when German bombers visited an ill-prepared Belfast on four occasions. South Belfast got off lightly compared with other parts of the city. Bombs fell in the Markets, damaging St. Malachy's Church and destroying Dunville's whisky warehouse; in Sandy Row ten people, gathered for a party, were killed when a landmine wrecked houses in Blythe Street. Nearby St. Aidan's Church also suffered (April 15th). The 4-5th May raid rained incendiary bombs on Stranmillis, forcing residents from their homes. Fortunately the tall chimney of the Bitumen Works was not hit: its collapse would have caused considerable damage to nearby houses. Churches prepared for raids by removing stained glass windows and valuable furniture to safe places in the countryside. Blackout was imposed. Tram windows were painted black and 'masks' reduced the light from car headlamps. Air raid shelters and static water tanks were built. Enterprising folk tunnelled into the 'clay hills' at Annadale to create their own, rather insubstantial, shelters. A barrage balloon was anchored on Robert Corry's green between the Crescents on University Road. Some people found a new item of furniture for the parlour, a Morrison shelter. For a time people sought refuge at night in the suburbs. The parishioners of Knockbreda were not impressed by the way such 'evacuees' treated their hall: a claim for damages was lodged with the Ministry of Home Affairs. The old Y.M.C.A. pavilion at Bladon also provided refuge. Children were evacuated to the countryside. Victoria College found a safer location at Portballintrae, Ashleigh House at Learmount Castle, Co. Tyrone. In 1939 Stranmillis College became a military hospital and the students took up residence in Fawcett's Royal Hotel, Portrush, where male students joined the Home Guard and trained with local service units. Staff had a new problem with the female students: protecting them from the amorous advances of British and American servicemen.

In 1944 the Ormeau Embankment was shut off and it and the Park became a huge camp for transport vehicles and American servicemen in preparation for the invasion of Europe.

Gardens lost their iron railings to the war effort. Schoolchildren could work their way through the army hierarchy by collecting waste paper, cardboard badges of rank being awarded according to the amounts brought in. Money for the war was raised through National Savings and the 'Wings for Victory' campaign. Living with rationing was a challenge and the more adventurous took to smuggling goods across the border.

The Balmoral showgrounds, which had been used as a Remount Depot in the Great War, and its buildings housed, among other things, an aircraft factory (Messrs Short Bros and Harland built chassis for Stirling bombers) and an American field bakery. The Belfast Corporation paid the R.U.A. the princely sum of one shilling a year for the priviledge of storing Auxiliary Fire Service equipment there. Belvoir Park was requisitioned and a jetty built for barges carrying munitions to the Admiralty dump established there.

The quadrangle at Queen's was divided up into allotments by the ingenious Dr Hunter and staff were encouraged to Dig for Victory. One such digger was Professor E. Estyn Evans. Hunter offered a cup for the best results but was suspected of not being even-handed in his administration of the contest. Stranmillis College gave up part of its playing fields for the same purpose. The cricket pitches at Ormeau Park were used for allotments and sheep grazed on the golf course prior to slaughter or shipment to England. A complaint to the relevant ministry about the "littered" state of the course got a dusty answer.

THEN AND NOW

A pre-Great War photograph shows a row of 'parlour' shops on each side of the middle Ormeau Road, the green groceries sold by two of them prominently displayed on the footpath in front. A woman and a man are chatting. Tramlines remind us of how many would then have travelled the Road. No tram is in sight. The only wheeled vehicles, apart from the woman's pram, are two carts whose horses patiently await the return of their drivers. Hurry, bustle? Certainly not.

Ninety years later the picture is very different. Buses a-plenty. Four lanes of traffic. Commuters hurry to and from 'luxury, executive' housing developments on the Saintfield Road, and indeed as far away as Ballynahinch, Saintfield and Downpatrick. The car has made a difference in deciding where we live and where we work.

A similar contrast might be made for the Malone Road. Stranmillis now seems less residential than 'restaurantial'.

Photographs in the Welch Collection at the Ulster Museum show slum conditions in pre-Great War Cromac. Raphael Street is cobbled, Riley's Court apparently only partly paved; wooden shutters on windows conserve heat; barefoot children line up for the camera; boot scrapers beside front doors point to dirty streets.

Today's Cromac is very different: modern homes by the Housing Executive, trees and shrubs to soften the streetscape. The sentimental will regret the loss of the character which the old Cromac had with its variety of shops, but it must be acknowledged that change has brought more gain than loss.

THE FUTURE

Transition, change, redevelopment are signs of vitality in a community. Of course not every proposal will be welcome. Too much may have to be sacrificed. A proposal to lay a road through Belvoir Forest to relieve congestion on the Ormeau / Saintfield Road was successfully opposed. Opposition to an hotel at Shaw's Bridge failed.

The Gasworks closed in 1988. Under the direction of the Belfast Corporation and Laganside Corporation, with European funding, the site was cleared, the work being awarded the 1998 RICS Award for the Reclamation of Contaminated Land. Office blocks and call centres are being built; an hotel is projected; a water basin with marine life has replaced the polluted Cromac Dock. According to the official brochure *"Roads and walkways reunite city, community and river"*. The Victorian office block is being restored and a new use sought for the spectacular 'Klondyke'.

Between Great Victoria Street and Sandy Row a major project is coming to fruition, the Lincoln Centre, comprising two hotels, office accommodation, a restaurant and a leisure centre, plus a carpark.

Finding a balance between preservation and change is a tricky business. It is our hope that those on whom future developments in South Belfast depend will manage to achieve that balance.

BIBLIOGRAPHY

Bardon, J. : *Belfast (1982)*

Batt, N. : *Belfast Sixty Years Ago* (Ulster Journal of Archaeology 1896)

Beale, G. and Phoenix , E. : *Stranmillis College* (1998)

Belfast Corporation : *The Belfast Book* (1929)

Benn, G. : *History of Belfast* (1877)

Blair, M. : *Once Upon the Lagan* (1981)

Brodie, M. : *Linfield 100 Years* (1985)

Carleton, T. : *Articles on Malone in U.J.A. vols 39 and 41*

Clarke, R.S.J. (ed) : *Gravestone Inscriptions, vol. 3 (Belfast), 2 (Down)*

Dewar, J. : *History of Elmwood Presbyterian Church* (1900)

Evans, E.E. : *The Site of the City* (U.J.A. 1947)

Farrell, M. : *The Poor Law and the Workhouse in Belfast* 1838-1948 (1978)

Jones, E. : *A Social Geography of Belfast* (1960)

Larmour. P. : *Architectural Heritage of Malone and Stranmillis* (1991)

Lindsay, H.S. : *History of St Bartholomew's Parish, Stranmillis* (unpublished)

Macaulay, A. : *St Brigid's Church, A Centenary Record* (1994)

McCreary, A. : *On With the Show* (1996)

McNeill, M. : *Mary Ann McCracken* 1770-1866 (1960)

Marshall, R. : *Book of Belfast* (1937)

Marshall, R. : *Methodist College* (1968)

Millin, S.S. : *Belfast Second Congregation, All Souls Church* (1900)

Newman, K. : *Dictionary of Ulster Biography* (1993)

O'Byrne, C. : *As I Roved Out* (1982)

Owen, D.J. : *History of Belfast* (1921)

Pilson, J.A. : *History of the Rise and Progress of Belfast* (1846)

P.R.O.N.I.: *Problems of a Growing City* (1973)

Rankin, P. (ed.) : *Malone House* (1983)

Robb, W. : *History of Malone Presbyterian Church* (1971)

Scott, R. : *A Breath of Fresh Air* (2000)

Templeton, G. and Weatherall, N. : *Images of Ireland: South Belfast* (1998)

Victoria College Centennial Volume (1959)

ACKNOWLEDGEMENTS

Thanks are due to, Ilse, my wife, for her helpful comments on the text; my daughters, Ingrid and Christine; the staff of the Local History Department of Belfast Central (Reference) Library; and Roy Allen, Dick McColgan, Marion McLaverty, Doreen Muskett, Maureen Wadsworth and George Templeton.

Dear Reader

This book is from our much complimented illustrated book series which includes:-

Belfast	Dundalk & North Louth
By the Lough's North Shore	Drogheda & the Boyne Valley
East Belfast	Blanchardstown, Castleknock and the Park
South Belfast	Dundrum, Stillorgan & Rathfarnham
Antrim, Town & Country	Limerick's Glory
Inishowen	Galway on the Bay
Donegal Highlands	Armagh
Donegal, South of the Gap	Ring of Gullion
Fermanagh	The Mournes
Omagh	Heart of Down
Cookstown	Strangford Shores

**Cottage Publications
is an imprint of
Laurel Cottage Ltd
15 Ballyhay Road
Donaghadee, Co. Down
N. Ireland, BT21 0NG**

For the more athletically minded our illustrated walking book series includes:-

Bernard Davey's Mourne   Tony McAuley's Glens
Bernard Davey's Mourne Part 2

Also available in our 'Illustrated History & Companion' Range are:-

City of Derry   Holywood   Ballymoney
Lisburn   Banbridge

And from our Music series:-

Colum Sands, Between the Earth and the Sky

We can also supply prints, individually signed by the artist, of the paintings featured in the above titles as well as many other areas of Ireland.

For details on these superb publications and to view samples of the paintings they contain, you can visit our web site at **www.cottage-publications.com** or alternatively you can contact us as follows:-

Telephone: +44 (028) 9188 8033   Fax: +44 (028) 9188 8063